OPERATION 'DRAGOON' AND BEYOND
THEN AND NOW

OPERATION 'DRAGOON' AND BEYOND

THEN AND NOW

Edited by Jean Paul Pallud

An Imprint of Pen & Sword Books Ltd

Operation 'Dragoon' and beyond – Then and Now
© After the Battle and Jean Paul Pallud, 2023

Published by After the Battle
An imprint of Pen & Sword Books Ltd
47 Church Street, Barnsley,
South Yorkshire, S70 2AS
Tel. 01226 734222
Fax. 01226 734438
Email: enquiries@pen-and-sword.co.uk
Website: www.afterthebattle.com
         www.pen-and-sword.co.uk

Printed in China by 1010 Printing International Ltd

ISBN: 9781399046114

Commissioning Editor: Rob Green
Editor: Jean Paul Pallud
Design: Paul Wilkinson
Cover design: Jon Wilkinson

Credits:
The three chapters of this book were originally published as articles in After the Battle magazine:
• 'Lieutenant Audie Murphy' by Winston Ramsey in issue 3 (November 1973);
• 'The Riviera Landings' by Jean Paul Pallud in issue 110 (November 2000);
• 'Audie Murphy's Distinguished Service Cross' by David McClure and Jean Paul Pallud in issue 110 (November 2000);
• 'November Push to the Rhine' by Jean Paul Pallud in issue 122 (November 2003);
• 'The Battle for the Colmar Pocket' by Jean Paul Pallud in issue 125 (August 2004).
These have been adapted and enhanced to produce this book and over 120 additional photos are included.

Acknowledgements:
The Editor would like to acknowledge the work of Jeffrey J. Clarke and Robert Ross Smith and thank them for the maps used from their publication *Riviera to the Rhine* and for the relevant citations made from that book. The Editor would also like to acknowledge the work of the US National Archives and the US Naval History and Heritage Command to collect, preserve and make available, documents and photos that represent the history of the US Armed Forces. Finally, the Editor would like to thank Winston Ramsey, who created the beautiful adventure that is *After the Battle*, and thus made possible the publication of so many remarkable stories.

Photo Credit Abbreviations:
BA – Bundesarchiv; ECPAD – Médiathèque de la Défense, Fort d'Ivry; USNA – US National Archives. Unless specified otherwise, all illustrations are from the After the Battle archive.

Front Cover:
Top: Operation 'Dragoon'. On D-Day of the invasion of southern France men of the 15th Infantry take cover behind a small rampart of sand shovelled up along Alpha Yellow beach at Pampelonne. (USNA)
Bottom: Today, the beach is one of the most famous on the whole Riviera. If you plan to check this comparison, be attentive and respectful because it could well be a nudist sector of the beach. In the background Cap Camarat with its lighthouse. (Jean Paul Pallud)

Back Cover:
Top: In July 1944, the 19. Armee guarded the Mediterranean coastline with three corps: on the left, near the border with Italy, the LXII. Reserve-Korps with two divisions; in the centre, the LXXXV. Armeekorps with two divisions; and on the right flank, from the Rhône River to the Spanish border, the IV. Luftwaffen-Feldkorps with three divisions. At Collioure, ten kilometres from the Spanish border, a 20mm Flak 30 gun protected the harbour. (USNA and Jean Paul Pallud)
Centre: Pursuit north up the Rhône valley. Between August 21-31, the Americans captured some 5,800 prisoners in the Rhône valley alone. Three of them, members of the Luftwaffe, were pictured in front of the First World War memorial at Loriol with a GI of the 36th Division. The memorial has remained remarkably unchanged. (USNA and Jean Paul Pallud)
Bottom: On February 8, after a final stand in the southeast corner of the Colmar pocket, the German command gave the 19. Armee the order to withdraw over the Rhine. In Colmar a dead German soldier lies prostrate in the snow in front of a garage where the Americans have emplaced two anti-tank guns. The author found that the picture had been taken at the major road junction where the Route de Strasbourg (behind the photographer) joins the Route de Sélestat on the right; off the picture to the left is Rue d'Ostheim. He took this comparison in 2004, just a year before the building was completely rebuilt, with its front part removed. It now houses a lovely pastry shop. (USNA and Jean Paul Pallud)

CONTENTS

INTRODUCTION from *Riviera to the Rhine*, by Jeffrey J. Clarke and
Robert Ross Smith 6

OPERATION 'DRAGOON' – THE INVASION OF SOUTHERN FRANCE
by Jean Paul Pallud 8

PURSUIT TO THE NORTH
by Jean Paul Pallud 146

THE BATTLE OF ALSACE
by Jean Paul Pallud 188

Scene on the Cavalaire beach on D-Day, with LCVPs from USS Andromeda (AKA-15) and Samuel Chase (APA-26). A group of German prisoners are passing beyond the LCVPs, and a smoke screen is developing beyond that. (USNA)

INTRODUCTION

THE OPERATIONS THE 6TH ARMY GROUP [with the Seventh Army and the 1ère Armée] constituted one of the most successful series of campaigns during World War II. Although opposed by many Allied political and military leaders from its inception and largely ignored by historians of the war, the campaign in southern France, including the 'Dragoon' landings, the seizure of Toulon and Marseille, and the battles for the lower Rhône valley, set the stage for the more significant ventures to the north. The subsequent pursuit north up the Rhône and Saône valleys, the drive northeast of Lyon to the Belfort Gap, the difficult Vosges campaign that followed, and the ultimate conquest of Alsace were critical to Allied military fortunes on the Western Front. Perhaps the greatest contribution of the southern invasion was placing a third Allied army group – one with two army headquarters, three

corps, and the equivalent of ten combat divisions – with its own independent supply lines, in northeastern France at a time when the two northern Allied army groups were stretched to the limit in almost every way.

Whether a third army group could have been supported by the Atlantic ports without an exceedingly lengthy struggle is doubtful, and without such a force the 12th Army Group would have had great difficulty holding the additional frontage from the Lunéville-Saverne area to the Swiss border. With the added strength of German units retreating unscathed from the Atlantic and Mediterranean, the German counterattack against the Third Army's exposed southern flank in September 1944 might have been far more effective, drastically retarding the initial Allied drive to the German border in the north. More important, Allied strength in northeastern France would have been much diluted without the forces of the 6th Army Group, and the Ardennes counteroffensive – or something similar – might have had a better chance of success or, at the very least, done more damage. In such a case the starting date for the final invasion of Germany might have been greatly delayed with unforeseen consequences.

Jeffrey J. Clarke and Robert Ross Smith, in Riviera to the Rhine

PART ONE: OPERATION 'DRAGOON' – THE INVASION OF SOUTHERN FRANCE

STRATEGIC DEBATE

In January 1943, the Allied Combined Chiefs-of-Staff met with US President Roosevelt and British Prime Minister Churchill at Casablanca for the 'Symbol' conference. The British argued that, with limited resources, it was futile to try to enter the battle in northern France at that point in time as there were not more than 21 divisions available to effect a landing on the Continent. Instead, they maintained that the Mediterranean presented the best prospects for success and pleaded the case for first knocking Italy out of the war. The Americans were not over-enthusiastic but, taking into account the fact that there was a large number of troops available in North Africa after the success of Operation 'Torch' (the invasion of North Africa), they preferred to go ahead with a landing in Sicily. The US Chief-of-Staff, General George C. Marshall, 'was most anxious not to become committed to interminable operations in the Mediterranean and wished northern France to be the scene of the main effort against Germany', and he complained that the Allies were by now planning the war on a day-to-day opportunity basis.

The Combined Chiefs-of-Staff met again in Washington in May 1943 for the 'Trident' conference at which the Americans proved willing to discuss possible operations in the Mediterranean in return for a British commitment to fix a target date for the cross-Channel attack. Agreeing that it might be too early to invade southern France, the Americans proposed to seize Sardinia and Corsica. The British expressed their doubts on the value of such an operation and insisted that any action in the theatre should be aimed at eliminating Italy from the war in 1943. The Americans finally approved this concept and General Dwight D. Eisenhower, then commanding Allied forces in the Mediterranean, was ordered to draw up plans for invading Italy with Sicily as a stepping stone. Launched on July 10, Operation 'Husky' attained an 'unforeseen degree of success'.

Early in 1943 the C-in-C West, Generalfeldmarschall Gerd von Rundstedt (second from right), came to see the Südwall for himself. The field marshal's convoy stopped at a vantage point overlooking the harbour. (Bundesarchiv)

Tourists in uniform on the Promenade des Anglais, Nice in the autumn of 1943. L-R front row: Generalmajor Walter Botsch, Chief-of-Staff of 19. Armee; General der Infanterie Baptist Kniess commanding Gruppe Kniess; Generalleutnant Otto Kohlermann commanding the Panzergrenadier-Division-Feldherrnhalle and Generalleutnant Kurt Hoffmann commmanding the 715. Infanterie-Division. (ECPAD)

On September 8, the Italian government recently formed by Marshal Pietro Badoglio capitulated. This the Germans had anticipated and when the Allied troops landed at Salerno on the morrow, they found them ready. On October 24, Eisenhower reported on the situation in Italy, making it clear that the Allies were facing a stalemate if not a serious reverse.

Beginning on November 22, under the code-name 'Sextant', a preliminary conference was held at Cairo between the British and Americans to prepare for a strategic meeting with the Russians. Here, Churchill stressed the British commitment to 'Overlord' – the invasion of France – but proposed to delay the operation for about six weeks so that landing craft scheduled to be transferred in Britain could remain in the Mediterranean long enough to sustain more amphibious assaults. The British proposed two directions for the conduct of the war in the Mediterranean: to push the offensive in Italy at least as far as the Pisa-Rimini line and to increase support to the Yugoslav partisans, including the establishment of minor beach-heads on the east coast of the Adriatic. If these actions meant a postponement of 'Overlord', they stressed that such delay had to be accepted. These proposals, which represented a return to British peripheral strategy and posed a serious threat to 'Overlord', might

The same group of Germans inspects the defences from the Ponchettes promontory. (ECPAD)

From the present-day Place du 8 Mai 1945, tourists gaze across the Baie des Anges.

have renewed the argument yet the Americans accepted them as a basis for discussion with the Russians.

The first plenary meeting of the 'Eureka' conference with the Russians was held at Teheran on November 28. Stalin immediately made clear the Russian point of view that the most suitable way to defeat Germany was an attack in north-west France, and that the campaign in Italy served no real purpose in this regard. Though he vehemently waved aside all Mediterranean operations, Stalin was much interested in the suggestion made by both Churchill and Roosevelt than an operation was being considered in southern France as a diversion for 'Overlord'. Not seeing this undertaking as a diversion, Stalin was pleased with the pincer aspect of two simultaneous landings on the north-western and southern coasts of France. Abandoned by the Americans, who derived great pleasure to find that the Russian views coincided with

Part One – Operation 'Dragoon' – The Invasion of Southern France • 11

The commander of Armeegruppe G, Generaloberst Johannes Blaskowitz, after a conference at the 1. Armee HQ in Bordeaux. The 1. Armee, with the LXXX. and LXXXVI. Armeekorps, had the task of defending the Atlantic coast from the Loire to the Spanish border. In August 1944, the army headquarters was sent to the Normandy front and the LXIV. Armeekorps took its place. (ECPAD)

their own, the British could find no room for manoeuvre.

Stalin's interest for the operation in southern France caught the Western Allies somewhat unprepared. Most of the planning staffs had remained in Cairo and from the material to hand (an out-of-date outline plan dating back to August), a study for a two-division assault was quickly drafted by the skeleton staff present. On the basis of this hasty study – and pressed by Stalin – Roosevelt and Churchill agreed to launch Operation 'Anvil' in southern France concurrently with 'Overlord'.

The former German HQ on Place de la Comédie is now an estate agent's office.

In Italy, the Allied advance had meanwhile bogged down. On January 22, a landing had been made at Anzio, south of Rome, but the Germans reacted vigorously and the invading forces soon found themselves confined to their bridgehead, unable to advance inland or even link up with the main body of US Fifth Army to the south. The Anzio venture began to consume resources earmarked for southern France. The British, more opposed to 'Anvil' than ever, pointed out that the battle in Italy was by then serving well the diversionary purpose for which 'Anvil' was intended, and on February 4 Churchill opened a strong attack against 'Anvil'. At the same time, the Americans reaffirmed their interest in 'Anvil' and a frustrated Marshall wrote to Eisenhower – now the Supreme Commander of Allied Forces in Europe – on February 7 that 'the British and American Chiefs-of-Staff seemed to have completely reversed themselves and we have become Mediterraneanites and they heavily pro-Overlord.'

Eisenhower had just started to plan for a three-division 'Anvil', in accordance with the post-'Sextant' directive from the Combined Chiefs-of-Staff. He held that 'Anvil' should go ahead for two reasons: to keep the promise given to the Russians and to make use of the forces available in the Mediterranean, particularly the French. Lack of shipping space prevented them from taking part in northern France so these forces would be wasted if 'Anvil' was not launched. Eisenhower, however, was becoming more and more concerned by the tightness of the landing craft allocation for 'Overlord' and on March 21 he cabled to recommend the cancellation of 'Anvil' as an attack timed to coincide with 'Overlord'. As a result, the US Chiefs-of-Staff reluctantly proposed to postpone 'Anvil' to July 10.

The approach of 'Overlord' froze the debate for a month but when the Combined Chiefs-of-Staff met in London on June 11 – five days after the landing in Normandy – the differences in the British and American position again came sharply into view. As a means to initiate planning, it was nevertheless agreed that a three-division assault should be mounted from the Mediterranean about the end of July. The need to secure more ports to support 'Overlord' soon added a new note of urgency to the debate, and the storm that severely upset the unloading schedule in Normandy made the need for harbours even more urgent. Insisting that 'France is the decisive theatre', Eisenhower argued that 'Anvil' was the most effective method to secure additional harbours, especially to bring in the French forces from North Africa. Furthermore, taking into account that the 'Anvil' forces would have to be supported from the open beaches for at least a month, and that in October the southern coast of France would be swept by the Mistral (a strong northerly wind), September 1 was seen as the latest date for executing the operation. In the circumstances, on June 23 Eisenhower recommended that 'Anvil' go ahead not later than August 30 and preferably a fortnight earlier.

Churchill, who continued to believe that the Allied forces in the Mediterranean would better be used in the prosecution of the Italian campaign, now appealed directly to Roosevelt. On June 25, in a lengthy memorandum which introduced few new elements into the debate, he pleaded strongly for Italy and against 'Anvil'. On June 28, Roosevelt answered that nothing could be graver than a deadlock of the Combined Chiefs-of-Staff and insisted that 'You and I must prevent this and I think we should support the views of the Supreme Allied Commander. He is definitely for Anvil and wants action in the field by August 30.' Churchill gave up the fight – at least for the time being – and on July 1, in the course of a telephone conversation with Eisenhower, he indicated that he would approve the operation. On the following day, the Combined Chiefs-of-Staff directed General Sir Henry Maitland Wilson, the C-in-C Mediterranean Theatre, to launch a three-division assault against the coast of southern France by August 14, reinforcing the amphibious assault with airborne units and following up with French divisions. The force was to seize the harbours of Toulon and Marseille, then exploit northwards to Lyon and beyond.

By early July, a new code-name, 'Dragoon', was chosen for the operation. (Such changes were frequently made in the fear that the previous code-name had become known to the enemy.) On July 12, in a note to Washington, the British Chiefs-of-Staff again queried the relevance of the operation, pointing out that neither they nor the British Government were convinced that a landing in southern France was the correct strategy. They nevertheless confirmed that they would do their utmost to make it a success. On July 19, Churchill cabled Roosevelt that the break-out in Normandy had opened new perspectives. He proposed to find a place along the coast of Brittany northward from Saint-Nazaire where a second landing could be made. From there, reinforcements from across the Atlantic could be easily introduced to the Continent. The Americans answered that they could see no gain in abandoning the carefully-planned Operation 'Dragoon' for securing what they saw as an unconvincingly better line of supply for 'Overlord'. On August 7, Roosevelt cabled that the landing in southern France 'should be launched as planned at the earliest practicable date and I have full confidence that it will be successful and of great assistance to Eisenhower in diving the Hun from France'.

In a meeting with the Supreme Commander at 10 Downing Street on August 9, Churchill made a final effort to convince Eisenhower who later recalled this discussion as one of the most difficult he had in the entire war. Churchill intimated that the Americans were behaving as 'a big strong and dominating partner', an argument which Eisenhower evaded by insisting that on military grounds alone, he could not yield. He suggested that if the Prime Minister had political reasons for backing operations in the Balkans, then he should approach the President. Finally, Churchill gave way.

Convinced that the Americans would not budge, on August 10 the British Chiefs-of-Staff instructed General Wilson to proceed with Operation 'Dragoon' and a directive of the Combined Chiefs-of-Staff confirming the instructions was issued the following day, just four days before the landing took place.

PLANNING FOR INVASION

Responsibility for planning and conducting 'Anvil' lay with General Wilson as Allied Supreme Commander, Mediterranean Theatre. Increasingly preoccupied with the situation in Italy, by late 1943 the Joint Planning Staff established by Wilson left the burden of 'Anvil' to the US Seventh Army, then temporarily based in Sicily. In December, the Seventh Army, then under Lieutenant General George S. Patton, was officially assigned to plan, prepare and execute Operation 'Anvil'. However, Patton soon left for England to take up his new posting as commanding general of the Third Army, together with his Chief-of-Staff and a number of key officers that Patton had chosen to take with him. So, Sicily was not the best place to conduct the planning for 'Anvil' and in January General Wilson directed Seventh Army to move a small planning staff to Algiers. Known as Force 163, this staff grew into a combined headquarters with American, British and French contingents.

In March, Lieutenant General Alexander M. Patch was appointed the new commander of Seventh Army. He immediately began rebuilding the depleted army staff with officers from IV Corps (which he had previously commanded), and he enlarged the planning groups at Algiers with more officers from the Seventh Army. In early July, having completed the reorganisation, he transferred the planners from North Africa to Naples where the united headquarters completed the planning for 'Anvil'.

In July, the Western Naval Task Force headquarters also moved to Naples. Created to conduct the naval and amphibious phase of the landing, it integrated

American, British, French and Greek vessels, and was under the command of Vice Admiral Henry K. Hewitt, the commander of the US Eighth Fleet.

The French units represented a sizeable part of the forces available for 'Anvil' and by mid-April, Général de Gaulle had unilaterally appointed Général Jean de Lattre de Tassigny as the commander of all the French forces involved. General Wilson compromised and agreed that de Lattre's Armée B would take command of the French forces ashore, but under the direction of the US Seventh Army.

At first, it was thought that the Seventh Army would assume a dual role as both an army and army group headquarters with the French army under its command, but, faced with the obvious problems that would inevitably arise from such a situation, it was soon agreed that an army group would ultimately be needed in southern France. This army group, which was to co-ordinate the two army headquarters, one American, one French, would be activated about the time that the 'Anvil' forces passed under the control of SHAEF. Early in July, General Wilson took the first step toward the formation of the group with the creation of the Advanced Detachment, Allied Force Headquarters, under the command of his deputy, Lieutenant General Jacob L. Devers. Devers soon made known that this detachment would be easily expanded into an army group headquarters and requested that he should be considered to command the army group. Eisenhower approved the idea and on July 16 Marshall made the appointment of Devers official.

It is interesting to note that Eisenhower and Devers had once been rivals. Both had graduated from West Point but, though Devers had entered service earlier than Eisenhower, the latter was now his superior in rank. Eisenhower's personal dislike for Devers was well known, as was his low opinion of Devers' abilities. When Eisenhower came to England at the beginning of 1944, Devers was commander of the US Army's European Theater of Operations and in charge of the build-up for 'Overlord'. He had been one of Marshall's leading candidates to command an army group within 'Overlord' but Eisenhower soon successfully recommended Lieutenant General Omar N. Bradley for the post. Also, while he requested officers who had served under him in North Africa (such as Patton) for combat commands in 'Overlord', Eisenhower persuaded Marshall to send Devers to the Mediterranean as deputy to Wilson. Though he realised that Eisenhower was trying to exclude his potential rivals, Marshall finally approved the transfer, accepting that it was only natural that Eisenhower would prefer to work with those commanders with whom he was familiar.

The long strategic debate over 'Anvil' had been a major problem to the planning staffs who tried to follow the political tide, drawing up a variety of invasion plans as the fortune of the operation waxed and waned. The earliest plans called for a two-division assault until Eisenhower called for a three-division operation in December 1943. In February 1944, Wilson assumed that the main operation would be of two divisions, with a third

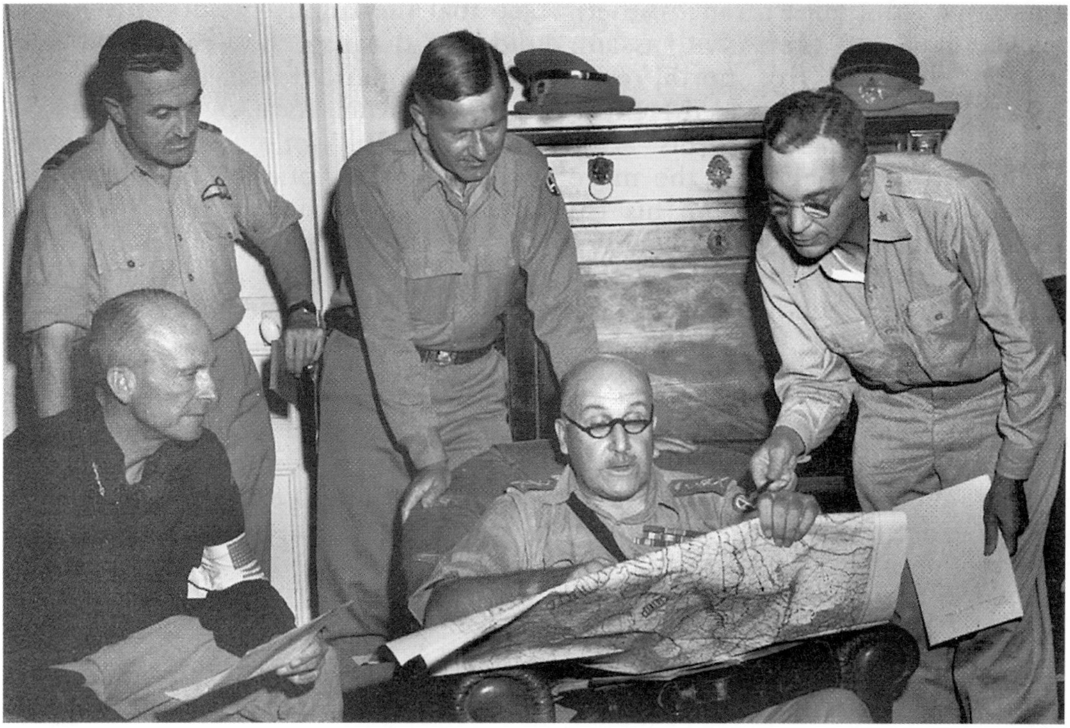

Planning 'Anvil'. L-R: Lieutenant General Alexander M. Patch, commanding US Seventh Army; Air Marshal Sir John C. Slessor, C-in-C of RAF forces in the Mediterranean; Lieutenant General Jacob L. Devers, commanding general North African Theater of Operations, US Army; General Sir Henry Maitland Wilson, Supreme Allied Commander, Mediterranean Theatre; and Major General Lowell W. Rooks, deputy C-in-C of North African Theater of Operations. (USNA)

Shipping in the bay of Naples prior to departing for the Southern France invasion. Two Italian light cruisers are present, along with dozens of US Navy and British amphibious and combatant ships. (USNA)

This photo of troops of the 3rd Infantry Division (note the division patch on the helmets) loading up in Bagnoli was taken on July 31 during a practice landing exercise. LST 603, LST 74, and LST 141 among others. (USNA)

LST's loading invasion supplies and vehicles at Nisida on August 9, just prior to the Southern France Operation. (L-R): LST 1019, LST 504, LST 1020 and LST 995. Passing by in centre distance is LST 505. (USNA)

LST's loading at Nisida on August 9. Ships present include (L-R): USS LST 550, USS LST 692 and USS LST 655. Note the barrage balloons overhead. USNA) following, and this plan was to govern the planning until July when the Combined Chiefs-of-Staff returned to the idea of the three-division attack.

At first, it had appeared that the best beaches for amphibious assaults lay near Sète, far to the west of Marseille, and along the coasts west and east of Toulon. The Sète area was soon ruled out, for this provided only limited port facilities, as were the beaches west of Toulon for they proved to be at the extreme range of the US XII Tactical Air Command bases in Corsica. The planners finally settled on the shoreline extending from Cap Cavalaire, about 40 kilometres east of Toulon, to Anthéor, 15 kilometres west of Cannes. This sector included minor ports such as Saint-Raphaël, Sainte-Maxime and Saint-Tropez, that might supplement the over-the-beach supply operations. Just to the west was Toulon, the first port objective that the planners hoped

LSTs loading at Bagnoli: LST 76, LST 286, and LST 174 among others. Note LCS(S) on bow davits of LST 286 and LCVPs carried by other LSTs. (USNA)

Part One – Operation 'Dragoon' – The Invasion of Southern France • 21

On August 8 the final loading of the assault troops began. Elements of the 45th Infantry Division embark in LSTs at Bagnoli. (USNA)

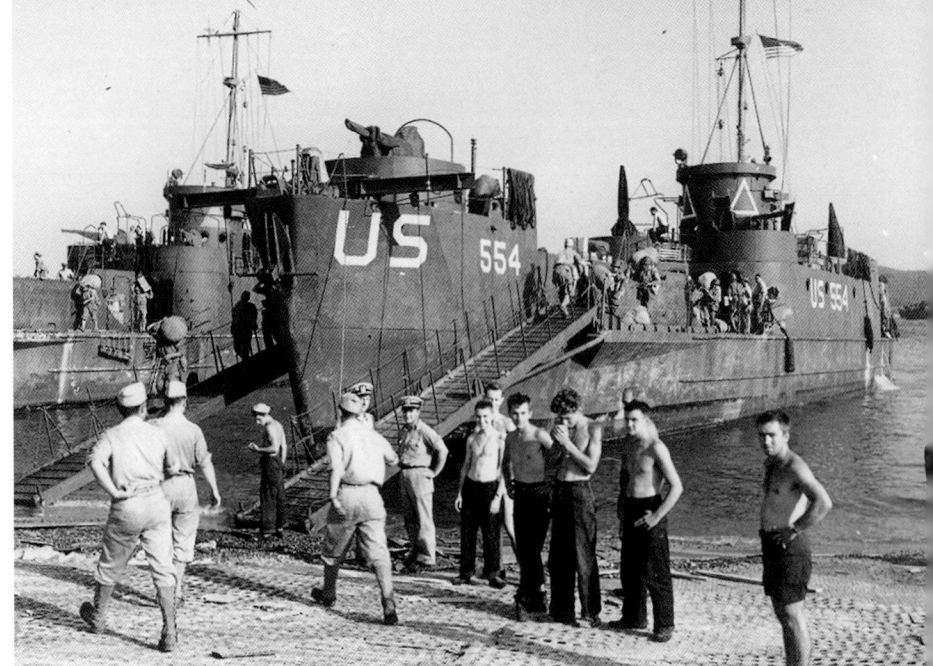

The 'Dragoon' D-Day convoys comprised over 880 ships and landing craft. At Naples, LCI(L) 554 waits for troops to board. (ECPAD)

Created in July to conduct the naval and amphibious phase of the landing, the Western Naval Task Force had its headquarters in Naples. The Task Force was under the command of Vice Admiral Henry K. Hewitt. This photo was taken in November 1942, when Hewitt (left, wearing binoculars) commanded the naval Task Force for the North Africa invasion. (USNA)

would fall by D + 20. Further west was Marseille, the capture of which was to take place by D + 40 to 50. The swift securing of the high ground that dominated the assault sector was vitally important and the planners had drawn the beach-head along the 'Blue Line' – an arc with a radius of roughly 35 kilometres from its centre at Cap de Saint-Tropez – which was to be reached as quickly as possible.

From early on, the planners had wanted an airborne assault to support the amphibious operation. By May, it had been decided that a full airborne division was to be used but the forces available by then amounted to no more than an Anglo-American regimental task force. Reinforcements were brought in from the States in May and June and by mid-July the airborne force assembled in the Rome area was about a full division strong. Its major elements were the British 2nd Parachute Brigade, the US 517th Parachute Infantry Regiment, three more American parachute and glider battalions and several battalions of parachute artillery. Seventh Army called it the

From mid-July, the 1st Airborne Task Force were assembling at ten airfields around Rome: the British 2nd Parachute Brigade, the US 517th Parachute Infantry Regiment, the US 509th Parachute Infantry Battalion, the US 551st Parachute Infantry Battalion and the US 550th Glider Infantry Battalion. On August 13, Sergeant Irwing Leibowitz, 163rd Signal Photo Company, pictured 1st Airborne Task Force Headquarters personnel kneel in prayer before boarding their glider early the morning of August 15. (USNA)

1st Airborne Task Force and selected American Major General Robert T. Frederick to take command.

The planners settled on nine separate landing beaches and laid down that the three-division assault was to be preceded by airborne forces jumping inland and by special forces operating on both flanks. Since the French units had no experience in amphibious warfare, they agreed that the initial assault should be made by American units.

From west to east, 'Kodak Force' – the main assault force under the VI Corps of Major General Lucian K. Truscott – was deployed as follows:

On the left, the US 3rd Infantry Division was to land on the Alpha beaches on both sides of the Saint-Tropez peninsula while in the centre, the US 45th Infantry Division was to land on the Delta beaches just east of Sainte-Maxime. On the right flank, the US 36th Infantry Division was to assault two Camel beaches on either side of Saint-Raphaël and the tiny Camel Blue beach at the head of the Anthéor cove, the easternmost beach. Each division was to be supported by eight amphibious DD Sherman tanks in the leading waves. Initially to serve as the VI Corps reserve and exploitation force, a combat command of the French 1ère Division Blindée, CC1 (this division used numerals to designate its combat commands), was to land on D-Day over the 36th Division beaches. (It should be noted that previous plans had been altered at the insistence of Truscott so that the most-experienced division, the 3rd Infantry Division, was now scheduled to land on the left, ready for an early drive on Toulon.)

'Garbo Force', the first French follow-up force, was scheduled to start landing over the 3rd Division beaches on D + 1. These elements included the 1ère Division de Marche d'Infanterie (1ère DMI, ex-1ère Division des Forces Françaises Libres), the 3ème Division d'Infanterie Algérienne (DIA), and the 1ère Division Blindée (less CC1 already ashore and another combat command to come later). The 9ème Division d'Infanterie Coloniale (DIC), with two infantry regiments attached, was to arrive by D + 9 and the rest of the IIème Corps d'Armée, including the last elements of the 1ère Division Blindée, were not to land until D + 25.

On the left wing, 'Sitka Force' – over 2,000 Americans and Canadians of the 1st Special Service Force of Colonel Edwin A. Walker – was to land during the night before D-Day on two islands, Port-Cros and Levant, which lay just south of Cap Cavalaire. Shortly afterwards, about 800 French Commandos of 'Romeo Force' were to come ashore at Cap Nègre, just west of Alpha Red, to destroy defences in the area and establish road-blocks along the coastal road to stop all German attempts to attack the beach-head from the left flank. 'Rosie Force', another group of less than 100 French commandos, was to land at the opposite end of the beach-head, at Le Trayas, and block the coastal road on the right flank.

Paratroops of the 1st Airborne Task Force were to jump in the vicinity of Le Muy, on the edge of the 'Blue Line', well before light on D-Day. Their mission was to clear the area for subsequent glider landings and to prevent the Germans from moving down into the beach-head through the Argens corridor.

THE FFI

Following the success of the landing in Normandy, the resistance forces in southern France had grown stronger and bolder in June and July. With Armeegruppe G concentrating its forces along the coast and sending unit after unit to the Normandy front, the FFI (Forces Françaises de l'Intérieur) had now taken control over large sectors of the interior. About 2,000 FFI soldiers had assembled on the Vercors, a rugged uplands south-west of Grenoble and established the République there on July 3 in the name of de Gaulle's Comité de Libération Nationale. Though they were poorly armed and equipped, the threat was alarming enough for the Germans to move in force against the Vercors in late July. On the 21st, 20 gliders brought in some 250 German paratroopers at Vassieu, right in the middle of the FFI mountain stronghold. Meanwhile, elements of the 157. Reserve-Division attacked the Vercors from the north and east and soon forced the lightly held passes. For hours, fighting raged around Vassieu but the resistance fighters could not retake the village. The fate of the battle was sealed on the 23rd when another flight of 20 gliders brought reinforcements to the paratroopers. A desperate call for help to Algiers fell on deaf ears and, as a result, the Germans gained control of the Vercors. Over 600 resistance fighters had been killed as well as around 200 civilians.

This major operation secured the Rhône valley for a while but it soon became clear that German forces were quite unable to subdue the resistance groups. Sabotage increased, bridges were blown and telephone lines cut, at a pace far beyond the capacity of Armeegruppe G to stop it or even repair the damage done. The Germans had to detach more and more forces to guard bridges and supply dumps and to keep open the main lines of communication, particularly northwards along the Rhône valley. Still, they had to resort to well-protected convoys to move safely. Communications between Armeegruppe G with its forces on the Atlantic coast and with Ob. West were frequently cut and radio links were only a poor substitute as the mountains caused interference. At the beginning of August, Generaloberst Johannes Blaskowitz, commanding the army group, reported that the FFI had now developed into an organised army in his rear. Basically, the Germans had by then lost control of southern France save for narrow strips along the Mediterranean and Atlantic coasts, the gap linking the two sectors through Carcassone and Toulouse, and the Rhône valley.

GERMAN DEFENCES

In early 1944, the German High Command had come to a reasonably accurate conclusion about Allied intentions in France, anticipating a major invasion somewhere on the Channel coast in the coming months. In January, they interpreted the Anzio operation as the first of a series of secondary attacks designed to tie down their forces before the main assault in northern France. Intelligence having revealed that the Allies had retained large uncommitted forces in North Africa, they also came to the conclusion that another major attack would be launched in the Mediterranean. In February, they had deduced that the assault would probably come in southern France, possibly before the main cross-Channel operation.

At the beginning of June 1944, the German forces in southern France were under the command of Blaskowitz's Armeegruppe G. In the west, the 1. Armee, with the LXXX. Armeekorps and LXXXVI. Armeekorps, each with two divisions, defended the Atlantic coast from the Loire south to the Spanish border. In the south, the 19. Armee guarded the Mediterranean coastline with three corps: the LXII. Reserve-Korps on the left with two divisions; Gruppe Kniess (soon to be redesignated LXXXV. Armeekorps) in the centre with two divisions; and the IV. Luftwaffen-Feldkorps on the right

All along the Mediterranean coastline, the Germans had taken over French coastal fortifications. Here, at Niolon, a fort facing Marseille across the bay was armed with four 120mm Modèle 1878 guns with a range of 10,7 kilometres. The 1. Batterie of Marine-Artillerie-Abteilung 611 soon took it over. (ECPAD)

After firing practice, the gunners relax for a peaceful evening. The Germans were soon to reinforce Stützpunkt Niolon and add four new casemates, each with a 90mm gun. (ECPAD)

Marseille, Prado beach. Early in 1943, the commander of SS-Polizei-Regiment Todt, Oberst der Schutzpolizei Bernhard Griese, surveyed the defences manned by his men. This second-rate unit was equipped with obsolete weapons like this MG26(t) of Czech origin. (ECPAD)

flank with three divisions. In addition, Armeegruppe G controlled the LXVI. Reserve-Korps which was holding, with part of one division and various other units, the area between the Pyrénées border and the Massif Central. Armeegruppe G also had the LVIII. Panzerkorps as a reserve force with three panzer divisions, one assembled near Bordeaux, another near Toulouse and a third near Avignon.

Though Armeegruppe G might appear reasonably strong on a map, grave shortages in men and equipment plagued all its forces. Most infantry

A new beach has been extended seawards, the old one of 1943 now having been filled in for a car park. In the background, the house that can be seen behind Griese's head is still standing.

A squad take up their positions behind the anti-tank wall built by the Germans along this length of the Prado seafront. The man on the left is armed with an old MP28/II, the second with a MG26(t). The same hill can be seen in the background of both wartime pictures. (ECPAD)

divisions were under strength and lacking equipment and even their staffs, at division level and below, were all undermanned. Also the drain on manpower had left most of the units with a high proportion of ethnic Germans from the Sudetenland, Poland and the Baltic States while many of the native Germans who remained were over age or physically unfit. The low quality of these divisions was brought to light by the designation 'reserve' that many of them carried. Even the three panzer divisions of LVIII. Panzerkorps were shadows of their former strength, being in various stages of refit and training.

In addition, several of the corps headquarters under Armeegruppe G were former training commands classified as 'reserve' corps. This designation was dropped in July or August although these headquarters never obtained the staff sections and corps troops necessary for effective combat operations. Armeegruppe G itself, which had become operational as such only in May, lacked many essential staff and Blaskowitz was unable to expand his headquarters: as its name Armeegruppe implies, the army group had an inferior status to that of a Heeresgruppe.

After the beginning of 'Overlord', the strength of Armeegruppe G gradually weakened as its best units were sent to the Normandy front. The 17. SS-Panzergrenadier-Division went first on June 7, followed by the LXXXVI. Armeekorps headquarters, the 2. SS-Panzer-Division, followed

At Cap Croisette, just south of Marseille, the Germans took over another French battery – Fort Napoléon – equipped with four 138mm dating from 1910. In June 1943, von Rundstedt paid a visit to the 6. Batterie of Marine-Artillerie-Abteilung 611 (132 men under Oberleutnant Friedrich Wurzer) which now manned the guns. With him are Konteradmiral Adalbert Zuckschwerdt in the post of Admiral Südküste (admiral, south coast) and General der Infanterie Hans Felber commanding Armeegruppe Felber. (Bundesarchiv)

Cap Croisette lies at the very end of the coast road south of Marseille.

Part One – Operation 'Dragoon' – The Invasion of Southern France • 31

One of the guns is loaded as a demonstration for the high-ranking visitors. In the foreground, one gunner carries the 138mm shell and another the propelling charge. (Bundesarchiv)

This view taken from behind the gun shows a concrete casemate on either side: on the left the one containing the propellent charges; on the right that for the shells. (Bundesarchiv)

by four infantry divisions, then four artillery battalions. These transfers were halted for a time but resumed in late July with the departure of LVIII. Panzerkorps headquarters, the 9. Panzer-Division, and yet another infantry division. They continued in August when the headquarters of the 1. Armee, the LXVI. Armeekorps and LXXX. Armeekorps left, followed by a regiment of the 338. Infanterie-Division, two more artillery battalions, and most of the anti-aircraft units defending the Rhône bridges. In the meantime, only the LXIV. Armeekorps came to replace the 1. Armee on the Atlantic coast, establishing its headquarters at Poitiers. Also, odd reinforcements were sent to southern France but these were mainly worn-out elements: two battered divisions from Normandy, one having to be merged with one of the reserve divisions guarding the Atlantic coast, and another division which had been decimated on the Eastern Front.

Three pieces can be seen in this picture showing No.1 gun firing. Its maximum range was 18,8 kilometres. (Bundesarchiv)

Today, the guns have been removed but the casemates can still be seen, as well as a superb casemate (of type H670) built by the Germans to house a 65mm gun.

At Les Lecques, five kilometres east of La Ciotat, a MG34 machine gun covered the coast. The turret from a PzKpfw II retired from service has been mounted on top of the casemate. (Bundesarchiv)

Six kilometres west of Cannes lies La Napoule where the Germans had established themselves in the château, a 14th-century castle nicely restored at the beginning of the 20th century by the American sculptor Henry Clews. Men of Ost-Bataillon 661 train their 37mm PaK 35/36 across the colonnade that faces the beach beside the château. In April 1944, this unit, made up of Russian troops, was to become the IV. Bataillon of Reserve-Grenadier-Regiment 239. (Bundesarchiv)

Changing the guard. (Bundesarchiv)

Today, La Napoule château and its art collections is open to visitors.

By mid-August, on the eve of Operation 'Dragoon', Armeegruppe G had lost one-quarter of its infantry divisions and two-thirds of its armour. Blaskowitz could expect no assistance from Heeresgruppe B, which was by then itself in a desperate situation; neither could he count on Ob. Südwest in Italy as it had never been envisaged to send forces across the Alps to counter-attack an Allied invasion in southern France.

The Germans were somewhat surprised when 'Overlord' was launched without a concurrent invasion of southern France but, nevertheless, they still had kept a wary eye on the Mediterranean coast. Guesses for the Allied amphibious assault fluctuated between the Italian Ligurian coast and the French Riviera but by early August most German planners were convinced that it would come in southern France. Considering that the most likely place was east of the Rhône, Blaskowitz decided to move the last armoured division to remain under his control – the 11. Panzer-Division – from the Toulouse area to the Rhône valley. By August 13, General der Infanterie Friedrich Wiese, the commander of 19. Armee, had himself concluded that the Allied landing would come east of Toulon and to meet the threat, he decided to move the 189. Reserve-Division and 198. Infanterie-Division, then west of the Rhône, across the river. These two weak divisions were to take responsibility for the static defence of Toulon and Marseille, thereby freeing the better 242. and

By early August, the Germans were convinced that another invasion, concurrent to 'Overlord', would come in southern France so Blaskowitz decided to move the 11. Panzer-Division to the Rhône valley. This picture was taken in Toulouse on August 13 as elements of Panzer-Regiment 15 were preparing to depart. (11. Panzer-Division)

It was August 19 when the 11. Panzer-Division started to cross the Rhône. The bridges had been destroyed by air attacks so the men and equipment had to be ferried across the river. (11. Panzer-Division)

We found that this uncaptioned picture was taken at Roquemaure, 12 kilometres north of Avignon. This particular bridge was hit by Allied aircraft on August 19. The suspension bridge which replaced it was built some distance upstream.

244. Infanterie-Divisions to be used as mobile reserves. However, with the complete destruction of the Rhône bridges by Allied air attacks, the lack of transportation, and FFI ambushes, these transfers were much delayed. By the night of August 14/15, when the ships of the Western Task Force were in sight of the Riviera, the move of these divisions across the Rhône had hardly begun.

By August 15, the sector of the shoreline about to be assaulted was held as follows. From the Toulon area to Anthéor, a few kilometres north of the Argens river, the coast was defended by the 242. Infanterie-Division of Generalleutnant Johannes Baessler. The division's left wing, the area that included the future 'Dragoon' assault beaches, was held by Grenadier-Regiment 765, the weakest of the division's three regiments. It had been formed only a few months previously and its fourth battalion was made up of Osttruppen – East European troops. Further east, the 148. Reserve-Division was responsible for the coast between Anthéor and the Italian border and one battalion (another Osttruppen unit) of its Reserve-Grenadier-Regiment 239 was positioned just to the north of the 765th.

In accordance with his fortress policy which aimed at denying entry to the Continent to the Allies, Hitler had ordered the strong garrisons at Toulon and Marseille to fight to the end. However, most of the defences of the two ports were facing seaward and there was now no time to fortify their land approaches.

This sketch, published by the Survey Directorate of AFHQ on July 31, 1944, showed the weakness of the German defences along the coastline of Southern France, here the Alpha Yellow beach: a single line of anti-tank mines and a double row of wire just behind. To cover it, there were only a few machine guns (arrows pointing downwards), two pillboxes and some trenches at the southern end (rectangle with a dot), and one pillbox at the northern end. Inland there were some areas of felled trees.

Part One – Operation 'Dragoon' – The Invasion of Southern France

On August 18, three days after the landings, an American photographer pictured the partially completed beach obstacles near Cavalaire. White tape marks suspected mine fields. (USNA)

This same day, an American sailor examines a 20-mm tank turret pillbox near one of the 'Dragoon' invasion beaches. This was a turret of a PzKpfw II. The PzKpfw II had been largely removed from front line service by the end of 1942 and the turrets were reused in specially built defensive bunkers. (USNA)

Later in August, a crew of USS Catoctin pictured another tank turret pillbox in the suburbs of Marseilles. This was a French APX turret from a Somua S35, it was armed with a 47mm gun. (USNA)

THE 'DRAGOON' BEACH-HEAD

As part of the Mediterranean Allied Air Force (MAAF) operations over southern France, air attacks indirectly related to 'Dragoon' had been underway for many months. In July, the air command was able to devote little effort to the preparation for 'Dragoon', primarily because of the demands of ground operations in Italy, but from the beginning of August a widespread air interdiction campaign was launched in southern France. To avoid the risk of identifying the assault area to the Germans, at first

The first phase of the air campaign directly associated with 'Dragoon' started on August 5, the attacks being directed at U-Boat bases, airfields and German communications in general between Sète and Genoa. From the 10th, the air campaign concentrated on coastal defences, radar stations and communications. At Anthéor, ten kilometres east of Saint-Raphaël, the large viaduct on the coastal railway leading to Italy was destroyed. Earlier, RAF Bomber Command had launched three attacks against it with the Lancasters of No. 617 Squadron: on the night of September 16/17, 1943 (12 Lancasters); the night of November 11/12 (10 Lancasters, each dropping one 12,000lb 'Tallboy' bomb), and the night of February 12/13, 1944 (10 Lancasters). None of the raids was successful and no direct hits were scored. (ECPAD)

By the eve of 'Dragoon', almost all important road and rail bridges over the Rhône and Durance rivers had been destroyed. This was the suspension bridge over the Durance at Cavaillon, 20 kilometres south-east of Avignon. (USNA)

On the D99, an ordinary concrete bridge has replaced the picturesque one destroyed in 1944.

the attacks extended from the Sète area all the way around to the Italian coast south-east of Genoa. From August 10, the air campaign centred on the coastal defences, radar stations and communications, during which phase over 6,400 tons were dropped so that by the eve of 'Dragoon' almost all important road and rail bridges over the Rhône and Durance rivers had been destroyed.

Meanwhile, the final loading for the seaborne elements had begun on August 8. Most of the VI Corps units embarked from Naples and Salerno, while the French 3ème DIA loaded at Tarento. The 9ème DIC boarded at Corsica but many other French units, including CC1, came directly from North Africa. The D-Day convoys comprised over 880 ships and craft and carried over 150,000 troops excluding naval crews and 21,000 vehicles. All convoys sailed as planned and the rendezvous were effected as scheduled.

RANGERS AND COMMANDOS

From 0.30 a.m. on August 15, the 1st Special Service Force landed as scheduled on the Levant and Port-Cros islands. The small German garrisons offered little resistance and the whole eastern part of Port-Cros had been secured by 6.30 a.m. All fighting was over on Levant by the evening but on Port-Cros, the Germans withdrew into old thick-walled forts. The heavy cruiser USS Augusta lent a hand but her 8-inch shells simply bounced off the walls and bombs and rockets launched by MAAF aircraft proved equally ineffective. Finally, on the morning of the 17th, HMS *Ramillies* lobbed a dozen rounds from her 15-inch guns at the fort which convinced the garrison that further resistance was useless.

On the mainland, the French Commando d'Afrique went in at Cap Nègre on time at 0.30 a.m. but the landing craft bringing them in had drifted westwards and the force went ashore some two kilometres west of its

At Cap Nègre, on the far left flank of the assault area, French commandos landed shortly after midnight on a rocky, cliff-faced coast. Though scattered because of a low haze which caused their LCA landing craft to drift westwards, they took the Germans by surprise and quickly overran artillery emplacements and pillboxes. (ECPAD)

We found that these pictures were taken on the south-eastern side of the promontory. In the background, Pointe de la Chappe.

Part One – Operation 'Dragoon' – The Invasion of Southern France

By the end of 1944, the war had still to be won and the new expanding French Army was in need of publicity. Consequently, it was decided to re-enact the successful operation by the Commando d'Afrique at Cap Nègre. The commandos had operated in the early hours of August 15 so no genuine pictures had been taken at the time, but, when the battle was restaged in January 1945, it was photographed in detail. (ECPAD)

objectives. Nevertheless, they quickly overran a handful of pillboxes and some artillery positions and by daylight had cut the coastal road as planned.

On the right flank of the assault area, another group of French commandos, the Groupe Naval d'Assaut, encountered considerably more difficulty. Brought in from Corsica aboard PT boats, the 67 men reached the shore near Le Trayas in rubber boats at 1.45 a.m. They started inland for their objectives but soon ran into a newly-laid minefield which caused many casualties and roused the Germans. By daylight, a few of the Commandos had escaped but those still trapped in the minefield were compelled to surrender. With ten killed, 17 wounded and 22 prisoners, the operation was a costly failure yet at least it had succeeded in diverting German attention away from the Camel beaches.

THE 1st AIRBORNE TASK FORCE

Reaching the airborne target sector near Le Muy, the troop carriers bringing the parachute pathfinder teams found the area completely blanketed by ground fog. From 3.30 a.m., the teams were dropped using navigational estimates and in consequence, most landed off their assigned drop zones. When the first serial of the main force came in at 4.30 a.m., they found no signals from the pathfinders and poor visibility over the drop zone. Nevertheless, the paratroopers jumped and, although half of the US 509th Parachute Battalion landed in or close to its assigned drop zone, the three battalions of the 517th Parachute Regiment were scattered far and wide.

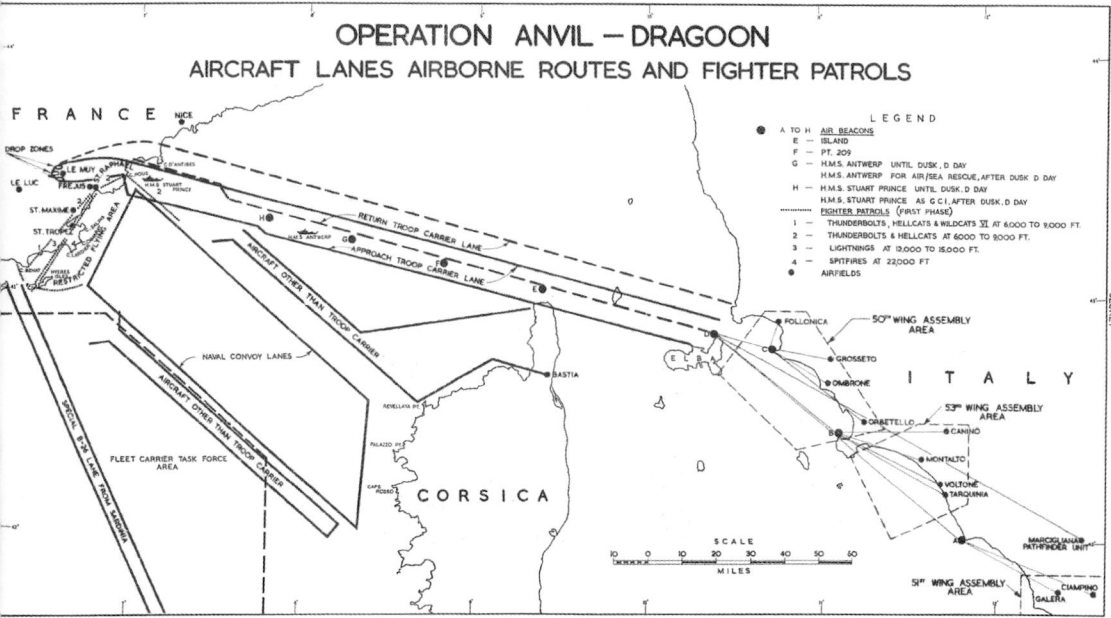

(Map from The Campaign in Southern France, Air Historical Branch, Air Ministry)

On the edge of La Motte, British airborne troops watch the gliders coming in. The C-47 tug planes are about to release the glider tow lines. As the road sign gave us a precise location, we easily discovered this spot on the eastern outskirts of La Motte although new houses and trees now make a comparison dull and meaningless. (USNA)

On the morning of August 15, C-47 transport planes lay a carpet of paratroopers over La Motte. This was a later serial of the main force, after the ground fog, which blanketed the area when the first serial came in at 4.30 a.m., had lifted. (USNA)

At the same time, from the ground near La Motte, Sergeant Irwing Leibowitz, 163rd Signal Photo Company, took this shot of the same grand scene. (USNA)

According to Sergeant Leibowitz's original caption, 'Leslie L. Rich, Company C, 509th Parachute Infantry Battalion, and fellow troopers move along a dusty country road toward their objective'. (USNA)

With two pathfinder teams signalling from their correct zone, things went reasonably well for the British 2nd Parachute Brigade which followed at 4.50 a.m. and two-thirds were dropped as planned, the remainder being scattered north-east and north-west of Le Muy. The paratroops struggled to orient themselves and regroup and by dawn some 60 per cent had assembled in the Le Muy area. Most of the others were scattered so far and wide that they did not join their parent units until D + 1 and the last men were not collected until D + 5.

With the best fields jam-packed with the first gliders to arrive, later pilots had to put their gliders down on rougher areas. Consequently, damage to the gliders was considerable but cargo and passengers were generally unhurt and by the evening of August 15, 90 per cent of the glider-borne troops and equipment were ready for action. All in all, nearly 9,000 airborne troops landed in Southern France on D-Day. (USNA)

German resistance in the sector was light and the paratroopers experienced only minor skirmishes as they moved off to their objectives and assembly areas. At La Motte, this squad deploys to cover the road to the village. In the centre, note the man with a beret: is he a member of the FFI or a British para? (USNA)

'American airborne infantrymen who played a spectacular part in the first day successes in Southern France are shown deployed along a road waiting for orders to move up.' A photo taken by another photographer of the 163rd Signal Photo Company, James A. Cuca. (USNA)

Such are the places where history was made.

Fog still obscured the landing area when the gliders bringing in the follow-up forces of the 2nd Parachute Brigade arrived at 8.15 a.m., consequently the pilots of the tugs turned back without releasing their tows and returned to airfields in the Rome area. The following serials were delayed about an hour and they came in to land successfully later in the morning. The gliders of the flight which had turned back in the morning returned in the evening and landed from 6 p.m. Confusion and some losses stemmed from the fact that the first gliders had landed on the clearest areas instead of their assigned zone so that when the

Part One – Operation 'Dragoon' – The Invasion of Southern France • 51

Men of the 509th Parachute Infantry Battalion taking a short break with some British paras. Because of poor visibility over the drop zone, the parachute units of the 1st Airborne Task Force were much scattered on landing, the 509th Parachute Infantry being particularly dispersed, only half of its men landing in or close to its assigned zone. Note the Union Jack armbands worn by the British soldiers, a means of identification rarely used by British airborne troops in other operations. (USNA)

later waves came in, they found their LZs packed with gliders and the pilots had to divert to rougher areas. After the operation, only 50 of the 400 gliders could be salvaged.

Except in Le Muy, resistance was light and the airborne forces came up against opposition only as they assembled and moved towards their objectives. German forces began to turn on the paratroopers later in the day but by evening the 1st Airborne Task Force had accomplished all its D-Day missions, save for the capture of Le Muy itself. Formal contact with the seaborne forces was made at about 8.30 p.m. when a patrol of the 45th Division met elements of the 509th Parachute Battalion south of Le Muy.

Near Draguignan, paratroopers dropped wide had cut all wire communications in sight, practically isolating the LXII. Armeekorps headquarters that was in the town. From then on, the corps commander,

On August 16 at La Motte, American paratroopers march German prisoners into captivity. Note how the three Germans in the lead march smartly in step. Shortly before noon on the 17th, major elements from the 36th Division began to arrive from the Fréjus area, thus ending the mission of the airborne force. (USNA)

This is the road to Le Muy.

Part One – Operation 'Dragoon' – The Invasion of Southern France • 53

On August 18, Sergeant Leibowitz pictured an impromptu Allied parley between a group of airborne soldiers, American, British, and French and enthusiastic FFIs. (USNA)

General Ferdinand Neuling, was out of contact with both the 19. Armee and his two divisions, his isolation being one of the major reasons for the German lack of reaction on the morning of D-Day.

THE MAIN LANDINGS

From 5.50 a.m. to approximately 7.30 a.m., the air force launched concentrated attacks in the assault area, 385 bombers and 900 fighter-bombers attacking coastal guns, beach defences and underwater obstacles. The Alpha Beaches were bombed by 83 B-17s and 138 Marauders and the northern section of the Camel Beaches was bombed by 162 Mitchells with good coverage. However, cloudy weather denied completion of the bombing plan in the Delta area and the southern section of Camel area was denied completion by similar conditions. Only 75 B-17s attacked out of 183 despatched. The medium bombers faced the same difficulties in the difficult

En route to the invasion of Southern France landing craft, as far as the eye can see, are spread over the calm Mediterranean on August 14, D-Day minus one. Photographed by crewmember of USS *Catoctin*.
(US Navy, Naval History and Heritage Command)

An invasion convoy en route to Southern France. It includes two escort aircraft carriers, the destroyer HMS *Tuscan* (right) and an unidentified British light cruiser (in left distance). Photographed by T/5 Brazle J. McCroby Jr. of the 163rd Signal Photo Company. (USNA)

Part One – Operation 'Dragoon' – The Invasion of Southern France • 55

Another invasion convoy, photographed from USS *Frederick C. Davis*, an Edsall-class destroyer escort. (USNA)

'Soldiers know it's the real thing when they receive invasion money prior to hitting the beaches.' Aboard a Coast Guard cutter, Lieutenant Richard Newell (right), aide to General John O'Daniel, the commander of the 3rd Infantry Division, passes out the currency to soldiers. (USNA)

On August 15, Signal Corps photographer James A. Cuca pictured troops, including a number of MPs, on an LCI en route to the invasion beaches. Note life jackets and US Flag arm bands, and the pipe frames around the 20mm gun positions to prevent firing into the ship's structure. (US Navy, Naval History and Heritage Command)

morning weather. In the narrative The Campaign in Southern France the Air Historical Branch, Air Ministry, gives the example of the 220 Mitchells and 191 Marauders scheduled to bomb gun positions between Cap Bénat and Anthéor; of these only 136 Mitchells and 152 Marauders bombed the target area.

The naval bombardment opened up at 6.50 a.m. At first, low overcast combined with smoke raised by the air bombardment generally forced the ships to resort to unobserved fire but the visual conditions improved after 7.30 a.m. and the bombarding ships moved closer inshore to concentrate their fire on the landing beaches. At 7.50 a.m., as the leading assault waves were approaching the shore, the naval fire shifted to the flanks. However, although the combined air and naval bombardment had knocked out some of the beach defences and cut paths across the obstacles on the beaches and in the water, it had generally failed to make an impression against the coastal artillery emplacements.

USS *Samuel Chase* (APA 26), a view looking aft in ship's LCM Number One. Note lightly armoured conning position, and the canvas-covered .30 calibre machine guns. (US Navy, Naval History and Heritage Command)

On August 13 Signal Corps photographer T/5 Allan G. Smith pictured church services for sailors and men of the 3rd Infantry Division on the forecastle of USS LST 4. Note the barrage balloons overhead and the 20mm and 40mm guns, with limiting rails around them to prevent firing into the ship's structure. (USNA)

A few days prior to D-Day, as the USS Tulagi (CVE-72) escort carrier steams through the Mediterranean Sea en route to the invasion of Southern France, Steward's Mate Second Class Miles Davis King carries a loaded magazine for a 20mm machine gun. (USNA)

On August 14 senior Allied officers posed for the photographer on the bridge of USS *Catoctin* (AGC-5), the operation flagship. (L-R): Brigadier General Gordon P. Saville, USAAF, air commander; Major General Alexander M. Patch, Seventh Army commander; Vice Admiral Hewitt, Western Naval Task Force commander; James V. Forrestal, US Secretary of the Navy; Amiral André Lemonnier, chief of staff of the French Navy. (USNA)

Operation 'Dragoon' was a three-division assault preceded by airborne forces jumping inland and special forces operating on both flanks. (Map from Riviera to the Rhine by Jeffrey J. Clarke and Robert Ross Smith)

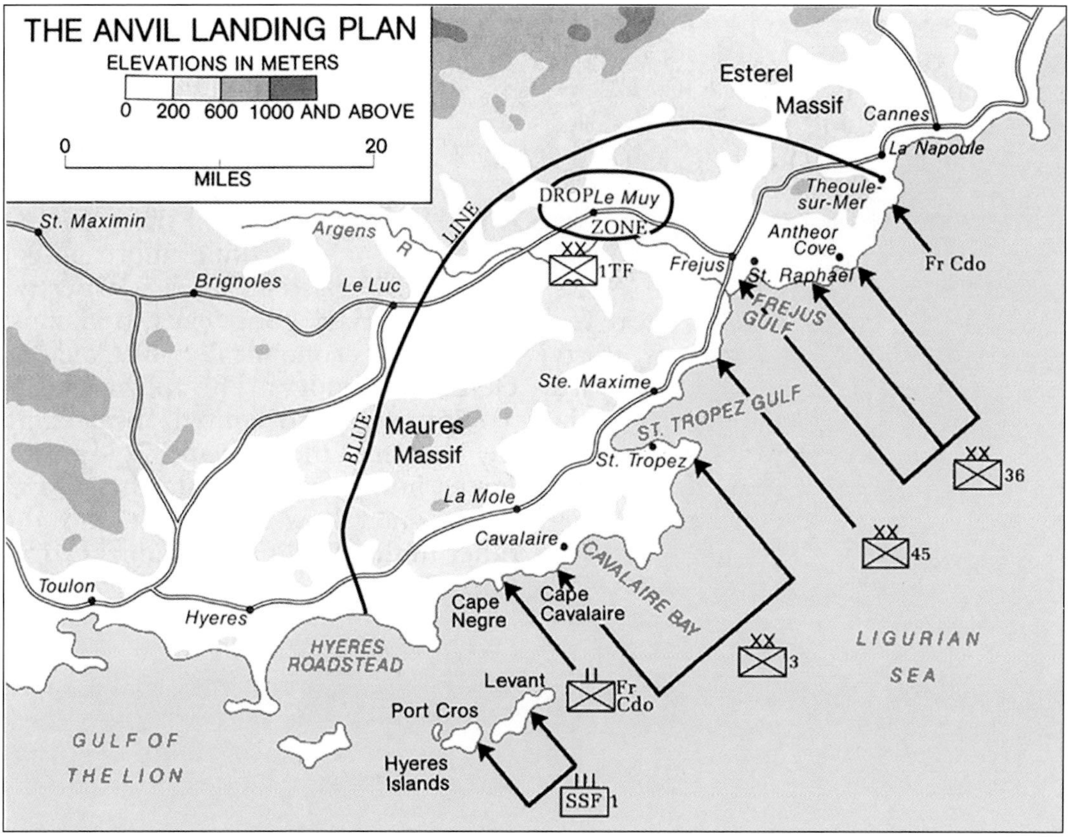

Part One – Operation 'Dragoon' – The Invasion of Southern France • 59

Heavy cruiser USS *Quincy* (CA-71) was part of the gunfire support group of the Alpha Beach Force. Two Vought OS2U Kingfisher floatplanes warm up on the cruiser's fantail prior to catapult launching. (USNA)

One Kingfisher floatplane is catapulted from the cruiser's stern. (USNA)

USS *Quincy* fires her forward 203mm guns off Toulon while supporting the invasion. Note smoke screen laid by the ship next ahead to prevent accurate counter-fire by German coastal artillery. (USNA)

On August 15, the light cruiser USS *Brooklyn* (CL-40) sent one SOC-3 Seagull floatplane to photograph results of shelling on the Cap Dramont sector, Camel Yellow. Note gun emplacements and other protected facilities in the target area. (USNA)

Heavy cruiser USS *Tuscaloosa* (CA-37) engages shore batteries off Cannes, with a destroyer at left and shells hitting between them. A photograph taken from light cruiser USS *Brooklyn*. (USNA)

View taken on August 18 showing USS *Gleaves* (DD-423) laying smoke off the beach-head. British light cruiser HMS *Dido* appears in the centre background. (USNA)

British LCAs head toward shore off Alpha Yellow Beach on D-Day. A photograph by Yale J. Lapidus, 163rd Signal Photo Company. (USNA)

From the 141st Infantry Regiment history: 'It was still dark as we climbed down the rope nets into the LCVPs. By the time we were loaded it was getting lighter but it was still quiet except for the sound of the boats scraping the iron grey sides of the ships as the assault boats rose and fell on the gently running sea. By 0630 hours we were circling; at first just the nine boats from one ship, then the circle grew larger and larger as more and more LCVPs were filled with soldiers. By now it was broad daylight and the coastline was visible in detail as the great invasion force swung into action. Wave after wave of bombers came in low and began to saturate the beach with their loads. At 0650 hours, the naval preparation started... Now our boats straightened out into a line of 'V's made up of five boats each. Suddenly the engines took on a new deep-throated roar and the square prows rose higher out of the water as we headed into the beach passing the slower LCMs, rocket-launching craft, amphibious 6x6s carrying 105mm artillery howitzers, patrol craft and finally the tiny minesweepers. At 4,000 yards we passed the last control boat and heard a young Navy officer on the bridge yell something through a loudspeaker... Now we were 2,000 yards offshore and the great rocket ships began to send their screeching cargo into the air. The sea was rolling lightly and the increased speed threw a fine salt spray into our faces.' (USNA)

An LCT approaches the 45th Division beaches north of Sainte-Maxime on D-Day. (USNA)

A column of Coast Guard manned LSTs moves toward the coast on D-Day of the invasion. (US Navy, Naval History and Heritage Command)

On D-Day of the invasion of Southern France, scene in the combat information center in the USS Catoctin, the operation flagship where plot screen has an outline of the area coastline on it. (USNA)

Senior officers follow the progress of the landings on a relief map aboard USS Catoctin. The map depicts the Alpha and Delta beach areas. Present are (L-R around the map): Amiral Lemonnier, French Navy; an aide; Vice Admiral Hewitt; British General Sir Henry Maitland Wilson; Admiral Sir John Cunningham, Royal Navy; Captain R.A.J. English, US Navy. Vice Admiral Hewitt has autographed this photo. (US Navy, Naval History and Heritage Command)

Boarding nets and LCVP alongside USS Samuel Chase (APA-26) discharging her embarked troops, 15 August 1944. USS Samuel Chase was part of Yellow Beach Assault Group Alpha Force. (US Navy, Naval History and Heritage Command)

As seen from USS *Tulagi* (CVE-72), the invasion convoy steams toward the objective area. Planes on the flight deck are Grumman F6F Hellcat fighters. The Carrier Force included two carrier task groups with a total of nine escort carriers: TG 88.1 (British) with HMS *Khedive* (24 Seafires, 899 Squadron), HMS *Emperor* (24 Hellcats, 800 Squadron), HMS *Searcher* (24 Wildcats, 898 Squadron), HMS *Pursuer* (24 Wildcats, 881 Squadron) and HMS *Attacker* (24 Seafires, 879 Squadron); and TG 88.2 (USN) with USS Tulagi (24 Hellcats, VOF-1), USS Kasaan Bay (24 Hellcats, VF-74), HMS *Hunter* (24 Seafires, 807 Squadron) and HMS *Stalker* (24 Seafires, 809 Squadron). The F4F Wildcat was initially known as the Martlet in the Royal Navy, and the F6F Hellcat as the Gannet, but they were renamed Wildcats and Hellcats in January 1944. (USNA)

Rear Admiral Calvin T. Durgin, the commander of TG 88.2, had his flag on USS *Tulagi*. The Carrier Force began operating soon after H hour on D-Day from a point about 30 miles off shore. At the end of the day the force retired southward. (USNA)

Officers on board USS *Tulagi*, planning the attack as the carrier nears the Southern France shore on August 15. (USNA)

On D-Day, USS Kasaan Bay (CVE-69) is seen through signal flags of USS Tulagi. As the days passed, it took up positions progressively further westwards as the emphasis of the fighting in the coastal sectors moved towards Toulon and Marseille. The third day it was based south of the Hyères Islands, and from D plus 3 to D plus 14 on a point roughly south-west of Marseilles. (USNA)

On D-Day, a F6F Hellcat fighter of VOF-1 is waved off during a landing attempt on USS Tulagi after a close air support mission over southern France. (USNA)

This same day, a Royal Navy Hellcat lands on USS *Tulagi* after a raid on an island off the coast of southern France. (USNA)

Part One – Operation 'Dragoon' – The Invasion of Southern France • 67

The seven Royal Navy carriers withdrew on August 24, but USS Tulagi and USS Kasaan Bay kept on launching tactical reconnaissance, the Hellcats and Wildcats also strafing convoys, troop concentrations, bridges, and railways. On August 16, in the Tulagi's ready room, Rear Admiral Durgin, (foreground) congratulates the pilots for destroying a target. Note chalk board message in background: 'be sure to charge guns on take off'. (US Navy, Naval History and Heritage Command)

Hellcats from USS Tulagi attacked a train in Southern France, leaving it in flames. One of the pilots, Ensign John A. Mooney, swooped back to take this picture following the rocket strike. Sorties began to diminish on the 27th, the two last fighter-bomber missions being flown on the 29th. Reconnaissance as far as Lyon having reported no enemy movement the two American aircraft carriers were withdrawn from operations on the 30th. (USNA)

A few LST were converted into makeshift aircraft carrier sporting a custom-built mesh airstrip above deck. The mini-carriers transported six L-4B Grasshoppers that were to take off and fly as artillery spotters. LST 286 can be seen left in this shot taken on August 15 from one of the three flight-deck LSTs used in the invasion of Southern France.
(US Navy, Naval History and Heritage Command)

During Mediterranean invasion rehearsal, Captain Brenton A. Duval Jr. demonstrated the use of the runway constructed of timbers and topped with metal landing strip mesh. The original caption indicates that conversion was accomplished in 36 hours and runway was 4 by 70 yards. (US Navy, Naval History and Heritage Command)

Pilots and spotters talk over their mission on the deck before taking off to serve as spotters for naval gunfire in August 1944, possibly on LST 525. (US Navy, Naval History and Heritage Command)

An undated photo of LST 906 with a L-4 Grasshopper just having left the flight deck, with Navy personnel looking on. (US Navy, Naval History and Heritage Command)

Part One – Operation 'Dragoon' – The Invasion of Southern France • **71**

ALPHA

On the left wing of the 'Dragoon' beach-head, three beaches had been allocated to the 3rd Infantry Division: Alpha Red and Green at the bottom of the Cavalaire bay and Alpha Yellow at the head of the Saint-Tropez peninsula. On the shores of Cavalaire bay, the landing zone consisted of low sand dunes backed by a narrow strip of pine trees with the coastal road lying beyond the pines. Cultivated fields stretched beyond the eastern half of the beach while rocky pine-covered foothills rose just inland to the west. About ten kilometers northeast of Alphah Red, at the tip of the peninsula, was the 3rd Division's other assault beach, Alpha Yellow. The landing zone provided over three kilometres of excellent beach on which the entire division could have landed but the sorties were poor.

The area was defended by elements of the IV. Bataillon of Grenadier-Regiment 765 (an Osttruppen battalion made up of Azerbaijani troops, formerly known as Aserbeidschanisches Infanterie-Bataillon 807) supported by two field artillery battalions and one coastal artillery battery.

Side by side, dozens of LCIs line up on Alpha Red as 3rd Division soldiers race up the beach. Both pictures were taken on August 15. Among ships present are USS LCI 592 and USS LCI 668. (USNA)

Men of the Alpha Force dig in on the beach immediately after landing on D-Day. (USNA)

Part One – Operation 'Dragoon' – The Invasion of Southern France • 73

LCVPs and LCMs pass LSTs while retracting from Alpha Yellow Beach on D-Day. (USNA)

Scene on Alpha Yellow Beach, with LVTs and LCVPs on the shore and a fire burning inland. The sign above broached LCVP says 'PA-52'. A photo taken by a Coast Guard photographer from USS *Samuel Chase*. (US Navy, Naval History and Heritage Command)

Troops and a Jeep towing a small gun land from USS *Samuel Chase* LCVP. Note the beach markers.
(US Navy, Naval History and Heritage Command)

Part One – Operation 'Dragoon' – The Invasion of Southern France • 75

Men of the Alpha Force dig in on the beach immediately after landing on D-Day. (USNA)

Troops from the 15th Infantry Regiment use the sand for cover as they await orders to advance. On the shoulder of the sergeant looking at the photographer is the divisional patch of the 3rd Division: three white stripes on a blue square. Another sergeant of the 15th Infantry – Staff Sergeant Audie L. Murphy – also landed here: he was to receive the Distinguished Service Cross for his role in overrunning a strong point in the hills overlooking the beach. (USNA)

Today, the beach is one of the most famous on the Riviera. We took this comparison in the spring, so as not to see it overcrowded with bathers and yachts just offshore as it would be in the summer. In the background, Cap Camarat.

Alpha Red, just east of Cavalaire. Sherman DD tanks have just 'churned up out of the water, instantly dropped the hood like snakes leaving their skins, and rumbled off down the beach with their 75s, blasting still belligerent minded German machine-gunners out of existence'... or so reads the 141st Infantry regimental history. A total of 36 M4A1 DD tanks were used in the invasion of Southern France, with the 191st, 753rd and 756th Tank Battalions. A total of 36 M4A1 DD tanks were used in the invasion of southern France, with the 191st, 753rd and 756th tank battalions. The DD Shermans encountered difficulties in Normandy due to rough sea conditions, but they had fewer problems in the calmer waters of the Mediterranean. (USNA)

Two Sherman DD tanks of the 756th Tank Battalion on the beach after being unloaded from LST 691 on D-Day. Note their collapsible skirts. LCM unloading truck at right is from USS *Arcturus* (AKA-1). (USNA)

A smoke screen is laid to cover D-Day unloading on Alpha Red Beach near Cavalaire. Note the men hunting for land mines on the far right, and the line of DUKWs heading for shore. (USNA)

An anti-aircraft machine gun half-track comes ashore from USS LCT 1144, in the Red Beach area on D-Day. Note the British LCT in the background. (USNA)

In the Alpha sector, 3rd Division, wounded are carried back to the beach on D-Day to be put on LCVPs. (USNA)

Wounded soldiers were soon evacuated from beach to LCVPs for transfer on to the hospital ship. (USNA)

French partisans went to the beach on D-Day, and became very friendly with the GIs. Note their FFI armbands. (USNA)

Shortly after 7 a.m., while ships were hammering the coast, radio-controlled LCVP landing craft loaded with high explosives, called Apex craft, were guided ashore on Alpha Red. Some crashed into the obstacles, opening channels as they exploded, others blew up on hitting the beach, detonating mines. Just before 8 a.m. 20 rocket-launching craft blasted the shoreline as the first troop-loaded LCVPs started their run-in, preceded by the DD tanks. The leading regiments hit the beach at 9.20 a.m. – the 15th Infantry on Alpha Yellow and the 7th Infantry on Alpha Red. Two LCVPs hit mines and sank, resulting in 60 casualties and, though the following waves landed as scheduled, mines, both offshore and on the beach, were a real nuisance, damaging more craft.

Ashore, opposition was weak and many of the Osttruppen began surrendering as soon as the attackers advanced beyond the beaches. On the left wing, having cleared strong opposition at Cavalaire by 10.30 a.m., the 7th Infantry made contact with the French commandos at Cap Nègre and began probing westwards. Other elements of the 7th Infantry pushed inland, taking Cogolin in the afternoon. On the right wing, the 15th Infantry reached Saint-Tropez in the afternoon, only to find that most of the town had already been cleared by FFI soldiers and mis-dropped paratroopers of the 509th Parachute Battalion. Having followed the 7th Infantry ashore on Alpha Red, the leading elements of the 30th Infantry pushed further inland and reached Collobrières in the evening, a whole day ahead of schedule.

On D+3, August 18, engineers lay a steel mesh roadway on beach Alpha Red. Note LCT 556 in left background. (USNA)

This same day, the scene at the Navy beach-master command post of Alpha Red. Note the visual signal lamps. (USNA)

Army anti-aircraft half-track emplaced by a beach exit road in the centre part of Alpha Red, August 18. (USNA)

A Navy LCT wrecking barge beached on Alpha Red. Note the broached LCVP and other debris in the background. (USNA)

LST 4 approaches the shore on August 16. USS Samuel Chase LCVP is in the right foreground. (USNA)

August 18. transports offshore, with barrage balloons overhead and an MP on the right. (USNA)

A DUKW nicknamed Beaufighter on Alpha Red on August 18. Note the French flag in background, and insignia on the DUKW. (USNA)

A DUKW nicknamed Beaufighter on Alpha Red on August 18. Note the French flag in background, and insignia on the DUKW. (USNA)

View from just off-shore of Alpha Red a few days after the initial landings. Lettered features: A: prepared beach exit; B: Bulldozer; C: Soft sand. (US Navy, Naval History and Heritage Command)

Following the landing of CC1 on Delta, 'Garbo Force', the first French follow-up forces, started to come ashore, some on the 3rd Division beaches near Cavalaire and the remainder in Saint-Tropez bay. Here on the beach at Beauvallon an LCI(L) unloads troops who appear to be from the French 3ème Division d'Infanterie Algérienne. Two infantry landing craft can be identified: LCI(L) 526 and LCI(L) 554. We have already seen LCI(L) 554 loading troops at Naples. (ECPAD)

Saint-Tropez lies in the background, on the other side of the bay.

AUDIE MURPHY'S DISTINGUISHED SERVICE CROSS

After landing on Yellow Beach, the 3rd Platoon, Company B, 15th Infantry was making this way up this road in the afternoon of August 15. (Jean Paul Pallud)

Some 200-300 metres further on the platoon came under fire from German foxholes about 200 metres away on the slope of the hill. This is the view from the German positions, looking south-eastwards. The American attackers advanced from the left background. Behind the vineyard, in middle distance running across the picture is the cane-lined ditch along which Staff Sergeant Audie Murphy made his way to the German foxholes. (Jean Paul Pallud)

The following is based on a report given in December 1944 by Sergeant Norman O. Hollen to accompany the recommendation for award of the Distinguished Service Cross to Audie Murphy: Crouching low, Murphy made his way up the ditch (left) with a machine gun until he was on the flank of the German foxhole (on the hillside in the centre). Laying the machine gun over the edge of the ditch, he fired a surprise burst at the Germans, killing two of them and silencing the position. He went back to return the machine gun and started again up the ditch in company with his buddy, Pfc Lattie Tipton. Two Germans then came out of the Bouis farm (right background) carrying a white flag and Tipton stood up to wave them to come whereupon a sniper shot him dead. Firing his carbine quickly, Murphy killed the two Germans. He then moved forward uphill and turned behind the German positions. In close combat, he wounded two Germans, killed two more and captured five. He sent the prisoners down the hill and started to return to his position in the platoon line when Germans suddenly ran out of the farm, trying to escape. Murphy fired at them, killing two, and six others surrendered. (Jean Paul Pallud)

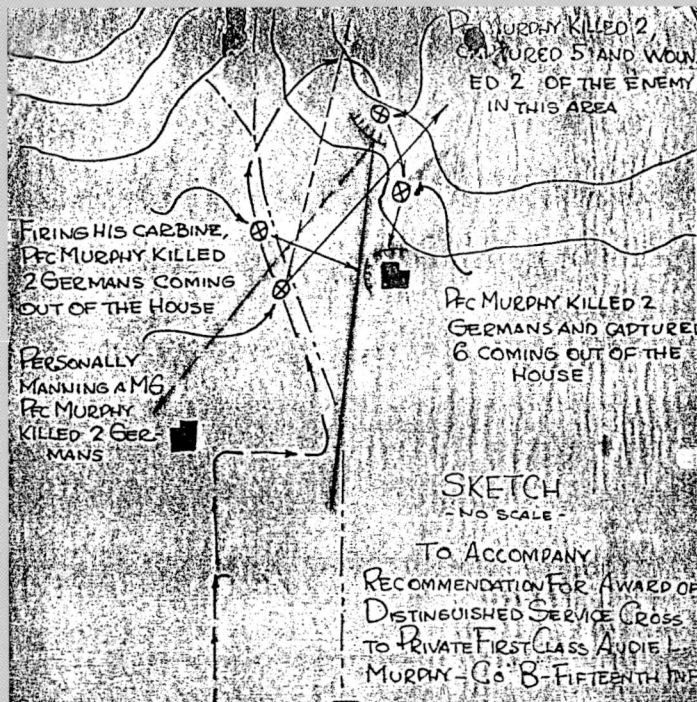

Having checked this sketch plan drawn for Murphy's DSC recommendation against a detailed map of the Ramatuelle area, the author finally succeeded in pinpointing the site of the action as being on the slope of the Bouis hill.

Firing a captured MG42, Audie Murphy re-enacted his attack at Ramatuelle for his biopic *To Hell and Back*. It should be noted that the eyewitness accounts do not mention Murphy's use of a captured German machine gun. It is hard to escape the conclusion that *To Hell and Back* is filled with products of the imagination. Another example is the story of him and two men attacking alone a 'huge German coastal gun'. The largest artillery on the Saint-Tropez peninsula belonged to Heeres-Artillerie-Abteilung 1193 which had three batteries of four sFH 415(f) 155mm guns. The AFHQ intelligence map puts one of these batteries in front of Ramatuelle and two south of Gassin but all three appear to have surrendered without a fight later in the day.

The Bouis hill today. On the slope a local who had played on the hill as a child and remembered trenches, foxholes and German graves, shows us the place where the German flak position had been. In the background one can see Pampelonne beach – Alpha Yellow. (Jean Paul Pallud)

On July 11, 1948, Murphy returned to Ramatuelle where the mayor, Mr Henri Battini, welcomed him on Yellow Beach. Murphy then went to the Bouis hill and there he found the grave he was looking for.

'The earth was mounded like a grave and at one end was a cross. A weathered German helmet hung from one arm of the cross.' So just who were these Germans willing to fight for the Bouis hill? The AFHQ intelligence map indicated merely a flak battery with two light gun-positions, both rated 'unoccupied', and four heavy ones, two of them 'unoccupied'; in addition, a single row of barbed wire surrounding the battery and two machine guns. When we wrote to the German Kriegsgräberfürsorge (war graves commission), their records stated there had in fact been three graves on the hill and three more elsewhere in the municipality of Ramatuelle. Those on the hill had contained the remains of Stefan Marczalkiewicz (rank not given), Gefreiter Friedrich Wowrosch and one unknown. These men must be the soldiers killed by Murphy (but note that the recommendation describes him as having killed eight). All six German graves at Ramatuelle were opened in 1959 and the dead reburied in the German war cemetery at Dagneux, near Lyon. Lattie Tipton was interred in the American war cemetery at Draguignan.

Men of the 45th Division march away from LCI(L) 513 which has just put them ashore and move out westwards in the direction of Sainte-Maxime. In the foreground, LCT 1143 is unloading wheeled transport. Note the two barrage balloons overhead. (USNA)

DELTA

In the centre of the beach-head, the 45th Division's delta beaches stretch along the shores of Bougnon Bay, a dozen kilometers north of Alpha Yellow and across the mouth of the Gulf of Saint-Tropez. Delta Red, the southernmost of the Delta's beaches, was located two kilometers north of Sainte-Maxime, and the others, Green, Yellow and Blue, were further up the coast, separated by stretches of 500 to 1,000 meters of inhospitable shoreline. Behind the beaches, the coastal road following the coastal contours led south-west to Sainte-Maxime and north to Saint-Raphaël. Rising, cultivated slopes led inland for about a kilometer before giving way to the steeper, wooded hills of the Maures.

This sector was defended by the I. Bataillon of Grenadier-Regiment 765 supported by a field artillery battalion and one naval battery.

There were no offshore obstacles on the Delta beaches and as the air and naval bombardment had silenced most of the defences, the 45th Division's two regiments landed without difficulty. Only a few rounds of mortar and some small-arms fire harassed the leading waves and the dispirited defenders readily surrendered as the invaders marched inland. Having landed on Delta Red and Green, the 157th Infantry advanced west toward

Delta Red today.

According to the original caption, LST 996 was the first tank landing ship to reach Delta beach.

A few hundred metres from Delta Red, at Cap des Sardinaux, soldiers of the 157th Infantry move westward. From here, Sainte-Maxime is two kilometres away. The 45th Division history The Combat Report of an Infantry Division describes the first hours ashore: '9.30. Orders from naval commander for all ships to close into the shore. We headed for Red Beach on Cap des Sardinaux. As we approached the shoreline we could see smoke from brush fires, blackened places, sites of bomb bursts, and some buildings slightly damaged. Then, as the details of the scene came into view, we could see the breaches in the seawall where the demolition crews had made openings for the assault platoons. In the water off Green Beach, we could see a tank with only the turret showing. One damaged landing craft was the only injured ship we could see. Initial objectives were quickly taken. Beyond the beaches the enemy's resistance was found to consist largely of covered road-blocks, sniper fire, and scattered uncoordinated pockets of resistance. The 157th fanned out and rapidly advanced inland and along the coast toward Sainte-Maxime. At 19.00, the 1st Battalion had taken two objectives and was north-west of Plan de la Tour with a motorised patrol on its way toward Vidauban. The 2nd Battalion had seized and secured its objectives, the 3rd had encountered no resistance on the beaches but was held up for a short time before taking Sainte-Maxime.' (USNA)

This is the N98 coast road as it appears today between La Nartelle and Cap des Sardinaux.

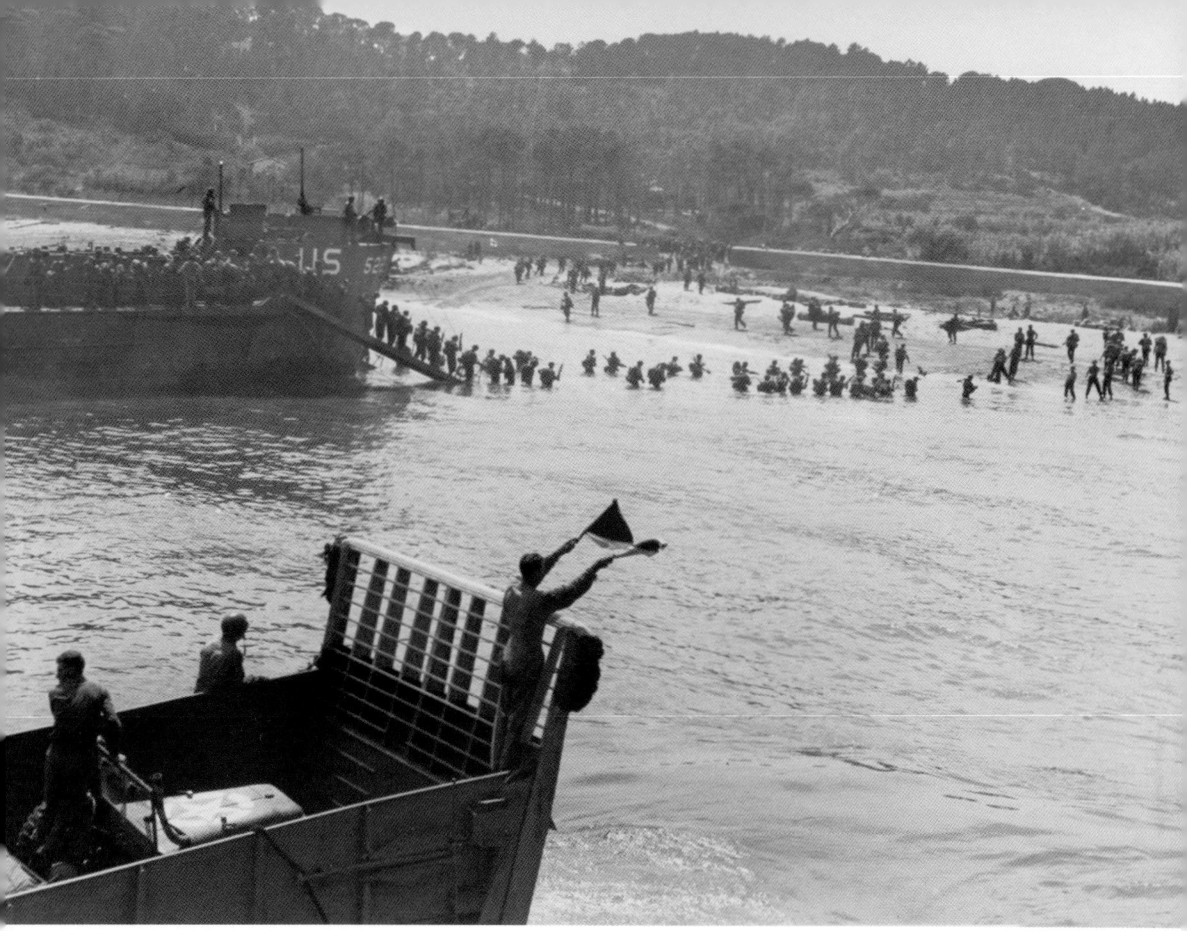

Troops landing from USS *LCI 522*, as the LCM in foreground prepares to beach near Sainte-Maxime on D-Day. Note the hole blasted in the seawall by engineers to facilitate movement off the beach. (USNA)

On D-Day, a navy beach-master gives directions to an army officer for the emplacement of his men after they had debarked from landing craft. Where precisely this photo was taken, is not known. (USNA)

Signal Corps Photo. Two soldiers observe a dead German soldier sprawled on the rim of his machine gun emplacement. (US

On August 17, medics care for wounded soldiers, lying on stretchers on the beachhead. (USNA)

On Delta Blue, another wounded soldier is carried to a Coast Guard manned landing craft for transfer to a transport lying off shore. (USNA)

Wounded men are carried on board a landing craft for transfer to hospital ships off the coast on August 16. The beach where this shot was taken is not known. (US Navy, Naval History and Heritage Command)

Part One – Operation 'Dragoon' – The Invasion of Southern France

On August 20, D plus five, LCTs – among them *LCT 198* and *LCT 559* – and LCMs land supplies on a Delta beach. Matted ramp in foreground is for DUKWs. In the background, the town of Saint-Raphaël. (USNA)

On August 26, a DUKW with a load of blood supplies and medical personnel, moves in from a landing beach. LCI(L) 18 is beached in the centre background. Note the Amphibious Forces insignia painted on the side of the DUKW. (USNA)

Unsolicited, these French civilians reported to the beach master on D-Day plus one and asked to be put to work to help unload the avalanche of supplies rolling ashore. This shot was probably taken on one of the Camel Beaches.
(US Navy, Naval History and Heritage Command)

Sainte-Maxime, brushing aside the weak opposition encountered on the way. They met stronger opposition in the town itself but naval gun-fire was called in support and by 3.30 p.m. Sainte-Maxime was secured. At dusk, contact was made with elements of the 3rd Division.

On Delta Yellow and Blue, the 180th Infantry also met negligible resistance, though four DD tanks were lost to mines on Delta Blue. The 1st Battalion ran into stronger resistance as they advanced northwards along the N98 coast road and in the evening the leading elements were halted in front of strong points at the southern edge of Saint-Aygulf, only half-way to Saint-Raphaël. Meanwhile, the 3rd Battalion had driven inland following a poor road over rough hilly terrain. They soon ran into strong resistance and by nightfall were still battling for the high ground about three kilometres inland. That afternoon, a recce patrol had pressed northwards from Sainte-Maxime along the D25 and had joined with the paratroopers near Le Muy by 8.30 p.m.

Commitment of the division's third regiment, the 179th Infantry, proved unnecessary and it assembled without incident near Sainte-Maxime.

Part One – Operation 'Dragoon' – The Invasion of Southern France • 99

CAMEL

On the right wing, three beaches had been attributed to the 36th Infantry Division: Camel Green and Camel Red on both sides of Saint-Raphaël, and Camel Blue at the head of the Anthéor cove. Two battalions of the 141st Infantry were to land on Camel Green, the division's primary beach, while the regiment's 1st Battalion landed ten kilometres to the north-east on small Camel Blue. The 143rd Infantry was to follow the 141st Infantry ashore at Camel Green and drive rapidly west through Saint-Raphaël to support the landing of the 142nd Infantry on Camel Red by 2 p.m. in the afternoon. At the head of the Fréjus gulf, Camel Red was a prize target for it promised to be the best beach in the entire landing zone for the disembarkation of men and equipment.

Camel Green. While men of the 141st Infantry disembark from LCI(L) 221, a bulldozer of the US Navy clears the roads leading from the beach to the N98 coast road some distance inland. In the background, Cap du Dramont.
(USNA)

Two tank landing craft, *LCT 1041* and *LCT 785*, unload DUKWs from the 540th Engineer Combat Regiment. (USNA)

Camel Green. As another LCT unloads its cargo of ambulances, the US Navy bulldozers continue clearing a path across the rocky beach. In the background lies Île d'Or (the golden island) where in the early 19th century, M. Auguste Lutaud had a tower built and dubbed himself 'King of the Île d'Or'. For 20 years, the eccentric Auguste I organised sumptuous parties on his small kingdom where the then jet-set of the Riviera had to be seen. (USNA)

Today, Dramont beach is another of the most popular beaches on the Riviera but Île d'Or is still privately owned.

D-Day on Camel Green, troops of the 36th Division come ashore. LCIs in the distance are the British *LCI 133* and *LCI 316*. Note the bulldozer working in the centre of the picture. (USNA)

The 36th Division's reputation as 'hard luck' unit seemed to be confirmed as its assigned landing area was one where the Germans had concentrated their main defences. That part of the coastline from the Argens river to the Anthéor cove was defended by the II. Bataillon of Grenadier-Regiment 765, backed by a field artillery battalion and one naval battery. Near Fréjus, the

D-Day on Camel Green, an M10 tank destroyer of the 636th Tank Destroyer Battalion comes ashore with a full set of wading trunks on the rock-strewn beach. Note the nickname *Babs* on the turret and *LST 49* in the background. (USNA)

III. Bataillon of the regiment was in reserve and the sector north of Anthéor was held by the IV. Bataillon of Reserve-Grenadier-Regiment 239, another Osttruppen battalion, this one comprising Russian troops.

Recognising the importance of the Fréjus sector, the Germans had built strong defences in the area. They had planted rows of mined tetrahedrons

Flanked by infantrymen, a gun-carrying DUKW rolls across rocky Camel Green. (USNA)

A few Ju 88s attacked the ships off shore on D-Day without achieving anything, but a small force of Do 217s dropping Hs 293 remote controlled gliding bombs had more luck in the evening. Just before 9 p.m. they skilfully approached the Camel beach area over the land so that the jamming ships off shore had to jam the glider bomb approaching head on, the most difficult angle for control. This photo of the wrecked *LST 282* was taken from USS *Catoctin*. (USNA)

The wreck of *LST 282* remains burned out and sunk off Camel Green, a photo taken on August 16. (USNA)

on the shoreline and built a two-metre-high anti-tank wall with a three-metre-deep ditch along its seaward side, as well as deploying two rows of barbed wire and extensive minefields. There were machine-gun embrasures in the anti-tank wall and several strong points just behind it. Five artillery batteries, ranging from 75mm to 105mm, dominated the beach and an anti-tank gun unit, the Artillerie-Pak-Abteilung 1038, had deployed about ten of the newest 88mm guns.

The 141st Infantry leading the assault landed on schedule at 9 a.m. against little opposition. Some machine-gun fire welcomed the first waves and sporadic shelling harassed the operation later in the morning but the Osttruppen surrendered as soon as the troops began to advance. By 10 a.m., the 141st Infantry had secured both Camel Green and Camel Blue, but on moving inland they came up against much stronger opposition.

The 143rd Infantry followed up without difficulty on Camel Green and turned westwards towards Saint-Raphaël and Camel Red. The leading troops met stubborn opposition from a series of strong points controlling the shore road and at 2 p.m., when landing was scheduled to begin at Camel Red, the 143rd Infantry had still not reached Saint-Raphaël. On the other side, the 45th Division could not assist as it was still five kilometres away. Consequently, the 142nd Infantry had to land on Camel Red without any of the scheduled support.

From 11 a.m., minesweepers clearing the approaches off Camel Red came under fire from artillery. Nearly 100 B-24 heavy bombers flew in just after midday, dropping about 200 tons of bombs on the German defences, but when the minesweepers tried to resume their job at around 12.30 p.m., it appeared that the aerial bombardment had failed to silence the German guns. The sweepers again retired while the naval task force – a battleship, two cruisers and four destroyers – opened up for a further bombardment. This also failed to silence the batteries and when the leading waves of LCVPs started toward shore, they came under heavy shell-fire. At 2 p.m., Captain Leo B. Schulten, commanding the Camel assault group, decided to postpone the assault for half an hour and informed Rear Admiral Spencer S. Lewis, the naval task force commander, of the situation. At 2.15 p.m., having been unable to contact Major General John E. Dahlquist, the 36th Division commander, ashore on Camel Green, Lewis directed Schulten to cancel the Camel Red assault and instead to land the 142nd Infantry on Camel Green which they did from about 3.15 p.m.

This decision was later strongly criticised by Truscott who termed it 'a grave error which merited reprimand at least, and certainly no congratulation' but his criticism appears unjustified for he based his judgement mainly on the fact that Lewis' decision delayed the landing of CC1. In fact the French combat command force landed over Delta beaches during the night of the 15th/16th and assembled ashore earlier than it would have done if it had landed over Camel Red on the 16th as scheduled.

During the night, the Luftwaffe attacked the 'Dragoon' bridgehead and it appears that one aircraft, a Dornier 217 of KG 100, succeeded in guiding a radio-controlled bomb to its target – LST 282 off Agay. The landing ship sank with 40 casualties and several pieces of artillery.

'Dragoon' had been a total success. Overall the casualties on D-Day were much lower than expected, with some 95 killed and 385 wounded. Churchill, who had remained firmly against the operation to the end, watched the landings from the destroyer HMS *Kimberley*. On the 16th, he cabled Roosevelt that 'everything seems to be working like clockwork here, and there have been few casualties so far'. This same day, he telegraphed King George VI: 'Your Majesty knows my opinion about the strategy but the perfect execution of the plan was deeply interesting'. There was no doubt, he added, 'that Eisenhower's operation made a great diversion. The fact that this is the precise opposite of what was intended need not be stressed at the present time.'

In the early morning of August 17, the Allies simulated a landing in the bay of La Ciotat with the objective of creating a diversion, hoping to draw German forces away from the main landing zones. US Navy Lieutenant Commander John D. Bulkeley proceeded to La Ciotat with a force comprising the USS *Endicott* (DD-495), the British gunboats HMS *Scarab* and HMS *Aphis* and 17 MGBs. While captive balloons saturated the German radars making them believe in a convoy, the ships bombarded targets ashore. The coastal batteries returned fire and then two German ships intervened, the UJ-6073 – the former Egyptian yacht *Nimeth Allah* – and the UJ-6082 – the former Italian corvette *Antilope*. They had just left Toulon and were en route to Marseille when they ran into the battle. Engaged by the two British gunboats, they returned fire and the Endicott opened fire in turn at 6.20 a.m. The close-range engagement lasted about an hour and the two German ships were sunk, the UJ-6073 at 7.09 a.m., the UJ-6082 ten minutes later. *Endicott* rescued 169 members of the crew, while *Aphis* and *Scarab* picked up another 41. This photo shows a large splash or explosion in the left distance. Helmets on the men indicate that this photograph was probably taken from a British ship, HMS *Aphis* or HMS *Scarab*. (US Navy, Naval History and Heritage Command)

This photo on USS *Endicott*'s bridge may have been taken after the 17 August engagement that sank the two German ships. (L-R): Lieutenant Commander Douglas Fairbanks, Commander of the Special Operations Group's Eastern Diversionary Unit, Captain Henry C. Johnson, Commander Special Operations Group (CTG 80.4) and Lieutenant Commander John D. Bulkeley, commanding Officer of USS *Endicott*. Another photo courtesy of Rear Admiral John D. Bulkeley. (US Navy, Naval History and Heritage Command)

This photo copied from a picture found on a German prisoner shows the *UJ-6073*, the former Egyptian yacht *Nimeth Allah* built in 1933. Reports from the Allied side tended to portray the two German ships as powerful corvettes but the La Ciotat battle was an uneven one, with the Allied ships having a very clear advantage. The final outcome of the engagement could not be otherwise. The *UJ-6082* was armed with one 100 mm gun and two torpedo tubes and the *UJ-6073* mounted only one gun, an 88 mm Flak gun. HMS *Aphis* and HMS *Scarab* had each two 6-inch (152 mm) guns while the USS *Endicott* had four 5-inch (127 mm) guns, two Bofors 40 mm guns, and five torpedo tubes (not counting the lighter anti-aircraft guns on all these ships). (US Navy, Naval History and Heritage Command)

View of La Ciotat harbour, showing results of Lieutenant Commander Bulkeley's diversionary force firing.
(US Navy, Naval History and Heritage Command)

Original caption indicates that this heavily damaged building was the German headquarters at La Ciotat.
(US Navy, Naval History and Heritage Command)

With hands aloft, German prisoners of war, mainly ethnic Germans from Poland, were passed to the rear under heavy guard on August 15. Note the landing craft in the background. (USNA)

The first German prisoners to be captured after the landing were taken to the beach on D-Day. (USNA)

A large group of prisoners is marched to the beach for transportation by ship to rear areas on August 16. This photo was taken by crewmember of USS *Catoctin*. (US Navy, Naval History and Heritage Command)

On August 18, on a beach in the Alpha sector, MPs organise German prisoners before they are evacuated from beach. (USNA)

On Yellow, Coast Guardsman Mortimer N. Judd and medic C.J. Wroblesi interview a German warrant officer who was captured on D-Day. (USNA)

Captured officers on board a transport off the invasion beaches on August 18. (USNA)

German prisoners of war, mainly ethnic Germans from Poland, on board a LCT, awaiting transfer to a Liberty ship, August 18. (USNA)

All attempts by the Germans on August 15 to mount a counter-attack against the landing area failed. They finally managed to assemble a force amounting to some four battalions of the 244. Infanterie-Division and they attacked from Vidauban at 7 a.m. the next morning. Half an hour later, they entered Les Arcs, throwing out the small paratroop force which held the town and gaining a foothold on the heights to the north. However, their success was short lived. The 517th Parachute Infantry dug in along the heights north and east of the town, the leading troops of the 180th Infantry advancing from Delta soon joined the battle, and by 3.30 p.m. Vidauban had been cleared and the German force in Les Arcs surrounded. Under the cover of darkness, the trapped Germans withdrew to the west. Later on the 16th, the paratroopers cleared Draguignan and captured part of the LXII. Armeekorps headquarters.

Meanwhile, on the VI Corps far left, west of Cavalaire, the 7th Infantry had pushed along the coastal road and by nightfall on the 16th, patrols were in Le Lavandou. Inland, the rest of the regiment met stronger resistance when both the German defences and rugged terrain delayed its progress. Just to the north, the 30th Infantry broke through a heavily wooded section of the

Pushing south-west along the coast from Camel Green, the 143rd Infantry encountered determined resistance and failed to take Saint-Raphaël by the designated time on August 15. Nevertheless, this was achieved by nightfall. Next morning a team of US engineers cross the bridge at the western end of the town. Another picture taken a few days later by the Signal Corps shows the concrete casemates seen on this side of the bridge being blown up to enlarge the passage. (USNA)

Maures mountains and by the evening of the 16th, the regiment controlled the main N97 road north-east of Toulon. On the corps' right flank, the 36th Division had by now secured the coast and pushed weak and dispersed German elements off the Esterel mountains. Having joined with the paratroops at Le Muy, the 36th occupied a broad area along the Blue Line from Théoule-sur-Mer to the Draguignan sector. In the centre, the 45th

Formal juncture with the 1st Airborne Task Force was achieved about 8.30 p.m. on the 15th when a patrol of the 45th Division moving north along the D25 mountain road met men of the 509th Parachute Infantry Battalion south of Le Muy. According to the original caption, these paratroopers (of the 463rd Parachute Field Artillery Battalion) walking through Sainte-Maxime on the morning of the 16th were the first paratroopers 'to get back to the beach area after their jump'. The marking on the truck on the left indicates that it belonged to the 157th Infantry Regiment, 45th Division. (USNA)

We found that this picture has been taken in the main street of Sainte-Maxime, now the Rue du Général de Gaulle.

114 • OPERATION 'DRAGOON' AND BEYOND – THEN AND NOW

Combat Command 1 of the French 1ère Division Blindée landed over Delta beach during the night of the 15th/16th and assembled near Sainte-Maxime. In the town, the local population surge around this half-track asking for food which the soldiers 'give out with great gusto' according to the photographer who took this picture the next morning. (USNA)

Division had cleared the area south of the Argens river from Le Luc to Fréjus. By the end of D + 1, save for its western part, the VI Corps' forces had reached and crossed the Blue Line.

German opposition had proved much weaker than expected. Resistance had been disorganised, counter-attacks weak and uncoordinated, and interrogation reports confirmed the low calibre of the German units facing the Allies. Eager to take advantage of the German weakness, Truscott quickly decided to begin executing

Another comparison found on the Rue du Général de Gaulle.

Part One – Operation 'Dragoon' – The Invasion of Southern France • 115

CC1 moved inland. A few hundred metres further along the coast road from Beauvallon, six of its M5 light tanks halt at the eastern entrance of Port-Grimaud. The bridge visible between the two leading tanks is still there today. (ECPAD)

While CC1 advanced inland, the 3ème DIA formed up to start the push westwards in the direction of Collobrières. These soldiers who have halted for a breather by the side of the N98A near Bertaud, three kilometres west of Saint-Tropez, are members of this division. Note the old-style French helmet of 1940 worn by one of them. (ECPAD)

Lengths of the concrete and steel barrier that lined the road were still there when we took this comparison.

the second phase of the operation – to launch an aggressive drive to the west and north-west – and, with Patch's approval, he issued the order before dark on August 16. The 3rd Division was to press on the west flank to the line of the Réal Martin and Gapeau rivers and hold there until the French IIème Corps d'Armée could reach it to continue the drive toward Toulon on or about August 20. To the north, the 45th Division was to push to the Barjols area, and in between CC1 was also to head westwards. On the corps' eastern flank, the 36th Division was to relieve the airborne in the Le Muy – Les Arcs area and then, leaving one regiment on the coast to cover the flank, was to assemble ready to advance north-westwards.

Passing a wrecked Luftwaffe truck, a French M5 half-track raced west on August 20. (USNA)

Scattered drops and failure of the gliders to land artillery and anti-tank guns had left the 2nd Independent Parachute Brigade insufficient strength to take Le Muy on D-Day as planned. The 550th Glider Infantry Battalion, together with elements of the 509th Parachute Infantry Battalion, undertook the task shortly after midnight on the 16th. They made little progress against stubborn resistance and withdrew by daylight. They started out again at 9 a.m. and, with artillery support, slowly pushed into the town. That afternoon, tanks of the 191st Tank Battalion moved down the mountain road across the Maures at which point the last defenders surrendered. (USNA)

Little changed in over 50 years.

On the afternoon of August 16, elements of the 157th Infantry, 45th Division, finally cleared Vidauban. Here, Private Aurelio Betancourt inspects a 20mm AA gun left behind by the retreating Germans. (USNA)

On August 17, members of Company H of the 180th Infantry try their best to repair a German car captured at Vidauban. (USNA)

After the failure of his attempt near Les Arcs, General Wiese concluded that it was now too late to mount a counter-attack and more important to establish a defensive line in front of the invaders in order to gain time to complete the switch of forces to the east side of the Rhône – mainly the 11. Panzer-Division and the remaining elements of the 198. and 338. Infanterie-Divisions. He assigned the responsibility for holding two lines of defence facing eastward to General der Infanterie Baptist Kniess, the commander of LXXXV. Armeekorps, the first line extending northward from the eastern defences of Toulon to Barjols, the second about 20 kilometres further west.

Nevertheless, the Allied advance was so swift that LXXXV. Armeekorps proved unable to even establish the first line of defence before the area was occupied, so on August 18 Wiese directed a general fall-back to his second line but even these plans were overtaken by events. By the morning of August 19, CC1 had reached Saint-Maximin, breaching the second defence line even before it was established.

On the eastern flank of the 'Dragoon' bridgehead, the Germans had retreated to the Italian border, so General Patch had no choice but to maintain strong holding forces along the Franco-Italian frontier. Made responsible for this front on August 20, the 1st Airborne Task Force pressed eastwards against no opposition and occupied Cannes on August 24. This picture of Cannes was taken two days later. Note the shell damage. (USNA)

Rue de la Rampe today.

Part One – Operation 'Dragoon' – The Invasion of Southern France • 121

Pressing on eastwards, the 1st Airborne Task Force drove through Nice on the 30th. Guided by a member of the FFI, this squad was pictured passing the Col d'Eze, a pass 512 metres high, eight kilometres east of Nice. (ECPAD)

Three kilometres further east along the Grande Corniche, the airborne troopers approach the junction with the road coming up from Eze. From here, the Italian border is about 20 kilometres away. (ECPAD)

This place is still the same today but the famous Grande Corniche (then the N7) has now been downgraded to the D2564.

Pressing on westward, infantrymen of the 3rd Division passed through unidentified French town. (USNA)

Charged with seizing Brignoles on the right wing of the 3rd Division, the 30th Infantry Regiment started out on August 17 with a fire-fight at Le Luc which was cleared after a four-hour action. These men of the 30th Infantry were pictured later that same day in Flassans, ten kilometres further west. In the background stands a Sherman tank of the French CC1. (USNA)

The N7 now bypasses Flassans leaving the main street a quiet and peaceful backwater.

The battle for Brignoles itself lasted until the morning of the 19th when it fell to the French and American attackers. In the town centre, Private Llyod Corun of Company F, 30th Infantry Regiment, takes it easy. German signs can be seen on the tree behind him. (USNA)

From then . . . to now and no change in this corner of Brignoles.

Part One – Operation 'Dragoon' – The Invasion of Southern France • 125

Advancing on the left of the 30th Infantry, in the centre of the divisional axis, the 15th Infantry reached Forcalqueiret, 12 kilometres south of Brignoles, on the 18th. These are men of the 2nd Battalion. (USNA)

We found that the picture had been taken on the D554 at the northern end of Forcalqueiret, looking south

GERMAN WITHDRAWAL

On August 16, faced with the Allied breakout at Avranches, the failure of his own counter-attack at Mortain, and the consequent risk of an envelopment of two of his armies in Normandy, Hitler agreed to the immediate withdrawal from southern France. On August 17, OKW (Wehrmacht High Command) accordingly issued orders to Armeegruppe G.

That same day, August 17, the Germans moved Maréchal Philippe Pétain, who headed the French government from Vichy (his seat of government in central France) to Belfort in eastern France, just 50 kilometres from the German border.

The OKW withdrawal orders were sent to Armeegruppe G in two parts on August 17. The first, pertaining mainly to forces on the Atlantic coast, was

On August 16, Hitler agreed to withdraw German forces from southern France and the following morning, the 19. Armee started to pull back northwards up the Rhône valley. None of this series of photos in the Bundesarchiv at Koblenz was captioned, but the author identified them as showing withdrawal of German forces from southern France. Never before have these pictures been accurately identified. (Bundesarchiv)

The same spot on the N7, about two kilometres south of Loriol.

received by Blaskowitz at 11.15 a.m. but the second, which concerned the 19. Armee, was not received at all that day. Communications were then in such a bad state that Blaskowitz did not get it until late on the morning of the 18th and by then Ultra decrypt sources had supplied Patch with a copy of the order. Thus the two opposing army commanders, Patch and Wiese, were reading the same order at the same time!

Upon receiving the first part of the OKW directive, Blaskowitz issued orders to General der Pioniere Karl Sachs, the commander of the LXIV. Armeekorps, who had been in charge of the Atlantic sector since the 1.

The author found that this shot, Frame 6 in the roll, had been taken in the centre of Loriol where another convoy of camouflaged vehicles had halted probably because the crossing of the Drôme river just north of the town was a bottleneck. The bridge there had been badly damaged during the night of August 16/17 when men of the FFI blew out 20 metres of roadway. (Bundesarchiv)

The N7 now bypasses Loriol but the Croix de Malte hotel is still in business in what is now a pleasant town freed of thundering traffic – then and now!

Frame 7 shows German engineers completing the construction of a bridge across the river at Livron, some distance upstream from the destroyed bridge. They were lucky that in the summertime, the Drôme falls to a low level. (Bundesarchiv)

Armee was moved north on August 10. He was to immediately assemble his force – about 70,000 men plus 10,000 civilians – and move eastwards south of the Loire river to join up with the main body of Armeegruppe G near Dijon. To be left behind were the garrisons of three port areas that Hitler had directed to be turned into fortresses and held to the bitter end: La Rochelle, Gironde Nord and Gironde Süd. Also, a small force was to stay in Bordeaux until the few U-Boats that were undergoing repair in the harbour could put to sea.

Blaskowitz did not have to concern himself with his far left flank on the Italian border as OKW had already transferred the 148. and 157. Reserve-Divisions to Ob. Südwest in Italy which was to handle their retirement to the Alps. However, to withdraw those parts of the 19. Armee that were engaged in the centre against the American and French invaders was a more difficult task. To ensure a swift move northwards up the Rhône valley, with the IV. Luftwaffen-Feldkorps on the west bank and the LXXXV. Armeekorps on the

The Drôme having been crossed, the withdrawal northwards continued. Transport was in short supply and many of the men had to walk up the seemingly endless N7. These two pictures, frames 11 and 12, were taken at Fiancey, five kilometres north of the river, and it was the sign on them which gave the first clue to the subsequent identification of the whole series. (Bundesarchiv)

east, Blaskowitz called for the latter corps to retire through three successive defence lines which were to hold the invaders east of the Rhône and south of the Durance river. Meanwhile, the 11. Panzer-Division and elements of the 198. and 338. Infanterie-Divisions that were west of the Rhône were to cross the river straightaway to bolster the defences against the advancing Allies. Detailed orders were issued, the first of the defence lines having to be reached during the night of the 19th/20th; the second during the night of the 20th/21st, and the third before daylight on the 22nd. As ordered by

Frame 16. The photographer was some distance to the north of Lyon when he pictured a camouflaged convoy which had pulled up under the protective cover of the trees lining the road. Two PzKpfw IVs of the 11. Panzer-Division face southwards ready to try to halt the Allied troops which the crews know are advancing towards them. (Bundesarchiv)

Hitler, the garrisons of Toulon and Marseille were to turn the ports into fortresses and fight on to ensure that the harbour facilities did not fall into Allied hands intact.

Though Patch knew from Ultra about the German withdrawal plans, he decided he could not act on the intelligence for the time being. For further operations inland, Patch believed that he needed the harbours at Toulon and Marseille, and on August 19 he made their capture the main army task. In consequence, he limited the western advance of VI Corps to Aix-en-Provence.

That same day, August 19, Blaskowitz withdrew his headquarters from Toulouse to Pierrelatte, about 50 kilometres north of Avignon, and for three days, while the 11. Panzer-Division strove to cross to the east bank of the Rhône on three ferries near the town of Avignon, he and his staff remained much concerned about an Allied drive to Avignon and across the Rhône. However, as a result of Patch's order, General Kniess was able to withdraw his corps without interference and all units pulled back on the final line of defence during the night of August 21/22. By the following morning, those forces scheduled to cross the Rhône from the west were on the eastern bank. On the 23rd, while the Germans withdrew their forces over the Durance and Blaskowitz moved his headquarters to Dijon, Truscott kept to his orders and cautiously limited the advance of the 3rd Division westwards, thus losing a superb opportunity to cut off a major part of LXXXV. Armeekorps south of the Durance. The remainder of Kniess' forces crossed the river during the night of August 23/24, and next morning Allied troops entered Avignon unopposed. The focus of operations was about to shift to the north.

TOULON AND MARSEILLE

Original plans had called for the first elements of the French forces to land between August 16-18 and the second echelon from the 21st. Seeking to take advantage of the German weakness, Patch decided to accelerate the unloading of the French forces and, in conjunction with de Lattre, he pushed up the schedule. The first echelon was landed mainly on the 16th which allowed the transport ships to return quickly to Corsica to bring in the second echelon on the 18th. By nightfall, most of the troops of the IIème Corps d'Armée were ashore although with only half of their armour, vehicles and artillery. Nevertheless, rather than wait until August 25 when all the vehicles and equipment would be landed, de Lattre proposed to attack immediately, asking only that CC1 be returned to him at once and that additional artillery ammunition be supplied. Patch agreed to the acceleration, released CC1, supplied the required ammunition, and at noon on the 19th, directed de Lattre to move toward Toulon and Marseille.

The original plan had been to attack Toulon and Marseille in succession but de Lattre, eager to press on before the Germans had time to reorganise, decided to move against both ports concurrently. Consequently, he divided his forces: the first group detached to attack Toulon along the coast while the second was to encircle the city from the north and drive westwards to

On a hill just east of Hyères, the Mauvanne battery comprised four 150mm guns in M272 casemates – [1], [2], [3] and [4] – with a command post in a type M262 casemate [5]. It was manned by the 3. Batterie of Marine-Artillerie-Abteilung 627 under Oberleutnant Ernst Gfrörer. (Google)

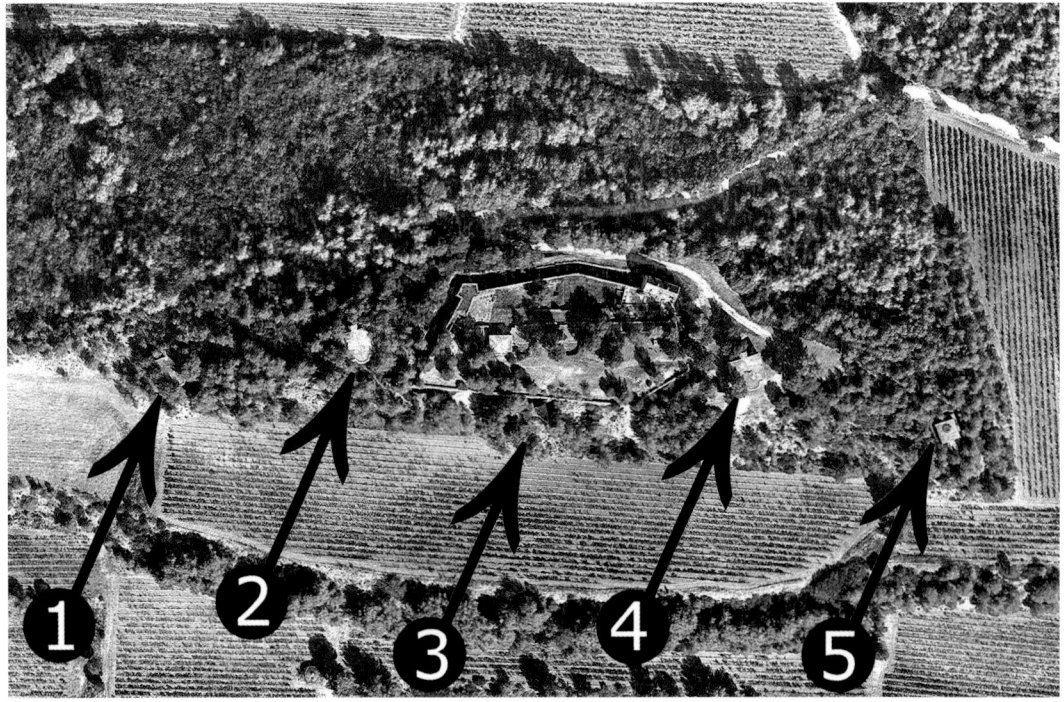

On August 19, men of the Commando d'Afrique assaulted the battery and captured most of its crew. As they did at Cap Nègre, the commandos later restaged their attack at Mauvanne for the camera. (ECPAD)

Though the gun has been removed, the pivot on which it was mounted can still be seen.

The guns that armed this battery, 15cm Torpedobootskanone C/36, had a range of over 19 kilometres. As the name implies, this weapon had begun its life as a gun for small destroyers but from 1940 it was diverted to coastal defence purposes. In this case, it was mounted in a casemate with its original ship's turret-like shield. (ECPAD)

Part One – Operation 'Dragoon' – The Invasion of Southern France • 133

This is the easternmost M272 casemate as it appears today. In front of it, a memorial recalls the commandos' feat of arms.

Marseille. Under Général Edgar de Larminat (commanding the IIème Corps d'Armée, not yet activated as a corps headquarters), the first group consisted of two infantry divisions (the 1ère DMI and the 9ème DIC) and some tanks. Under Général Aimé de Monsabert, the 3ème DIA commander, the second group comprised the 3ème DIA and CC1.

The German garrison in Toulon consisted of about 18,000 men, of whom nearly 3,000 were Luftwaffe and 5,500 naval personnel, plus naval and army artillery and anti-aircraft batteries. The large harbour was surrounded by rugged hills and, given time, could have been turned into a formidable fortress but the defences were strongest in the wrong places and the defenders lacked time to reorganise.

The battery fire was controlled from a two-story M262 Feuerleitstand (fire control post). At Mauvanne, the M262 bunker – eight metres high, 11 metres wide and 17 metres long – is now largely hidden by bushes and trees.

At the rear of the bunker, two staircases provide access to the lower level, the main room of the control post, from which distance and other data were calculated and transmitted to the gunners. Another M262 Feuerleitstand, the one atop the cliff at Longues-sur-Mer in Normandy, played a major role in the famous film 'The Longest Day': it was there that the scene was filmed when, in the early morning of June 6, Major Werner Pluskat sees Allied ships suddenly and silently emerge out of the fog, an entire line of them, all across the horizon.

However, the swift French advance had cut off Generalleutnant Johannes Baessler, the garrison commander, from the city and Konteradmiral Heinrich Ruhfus, the Sea Commander French Riviera, had to take command. He did his best to strengthen the weak sectors north and west of the city and also decided to evacuate the civilian population of some 100,000 men, women and children.

The French invested Toulon on the morning of August 20. Attacking from the east, de Larminat's force met strong resistance and advanced slowly, reducing a series of strong points one by one. In the north, although advancing across rough mountains, de Monsabert had an easier time and his men succeeded in outflanking the German defences. While the 3ème Régiment de Spahis Algériens completed the encirclement of Toulon from the north and west, de Monsabert's leading elements pressed westwards and soon reached strongly-defended Aubagne, the key to the eastern approaches to Marseille. De Larminat renewed his attack on Toulon with energy on the 21st but progress was disappointing in front of stiffening resistance. One tank company succeeded in breaking through and penetrating to about five kilometres from the centre of the city but it was soon cut off; holding out for 36 hours, they took heavy casualties.

In the evening of the 21st, an argument broke out between de Lattre and de Larminat. The latter wanted to take command of the entire operation against Toulon and Marseille with his IIème Corps d'Armée but de Lattre refused and, after a heated discussion, dismissed de Larminat and took direct control of the operation himself.

Day after day, French pressure against Toulon increased; strong points were overrun one after another, and slowly the defenders were forced back into the inner fortifications. Isolated groups resisting in the forts

Having silenced a 75mm anti-tank gun in the Avenue du XVème Corps in the western part of Toulon, French soldiers proceed to tow the gun into a suitable position to turn it against the Germans. One of the German crew lies dead in the foreground. (ECPAD)

overlooking the town were persuaded to surrender and the German defences progressively lost cohesion until the last organised resistance in the town ended on August 26. After two days of intense air and naval bombardment, Admiral Ruhfus surrendered on the morning of the 28th together with 2,500 men on the Saint-Mandrier peninsula across the harbour. Toulon had been secured a full week ahead of schedule and the French reported to have taken 17,000 prisoners.

Under Generalleutnant Hans Schaefer, the commander of the 244. Infanterie-Division, the Marseille garrison amounted to about 13,000 men, including nearly 4,000 Luftwaffe and 2,500 Kriegsmarine personnel, most of the remainder being from the 244. Infanterie-Division. The land approaches to the city favoured the defenders but, again, lack of time and equipment precluded the Germans from building fortifications; in fact, they were even less extensive than those at Toulon. As the French forces came closer, the FFI inside the city became bolder. At the same time, the inhabitants – some half a million – were becoming increasingly hostile and on the morning of August 22 a major uprising broke out in the city.

Meanwhile, having probed aggressively to the west, de Monsabert had come across German forces holding out in strength at Aubagne, just east of

Toulon fell on August 26 and the French lost no time to celebrate its liberation. Already the same day, Jeeps, half-tracks and an M8 howitzer motor carriage paraded through Place Gabriel Péri. In the background we can see some M3A1 scout cars, a type that had been retired from US Army service but was still widely used in the French units at the time. (USNA)

Marseille. He ordered the position to be bypassed and on the 22nd his forces were approaching the northern and eastern outskirts of the city. By the evening, the French were within eight kilometres of the heart of the city and making preparations to assault the harbour area the following day. However, concerned about the dispersal of his forces and the lack of supplies, de Lattre warned de Monsabert not to begin a full battle for the city and to limit his attack to clearing the suburbs until more forces arrived. De Monsabert obeyed the order with 'flexibility' and did not prevent elements of the 7ème Régiment de Tirailleurs Algériens from breaking into the eastern suburbs

The Palais de Justice stands in the left background, then as now.

Probing westwards, the French vanguard came across the strongly defended town of Aubagne, the key to the eastern approach to Marseille, but bypassed the positions by diverting to the south. Here, infantry of the 7ème Régiment de Tirailleurs Algériens and tanks of CC1 arriving from Gémenos advance on the N96. (ECPAD)

Now renumbered the N396, this stretch of road has changed little since 1944. In the background, the western extremity of the famous Sainte-Baume mountain.

of Marseille in the early hours of the 23rd. Encouraged by crowds of exuberant civilians, the leading troops made for the city centre and by 10 a.m. had reached the harbour area. Later in the day, the rest of the regiment and tanks of CC1 followed from the north. For the next three days, while more French forces were brought in, the battle in the city turned into a house-to-house and strong point-to-strong point fight. Finally, on the evening of August 27, Schaefer agreed to discuss terms with de Monsabert and a formal surrender came into being at 1 p.m., August 28 – the same day Toulon fell. The French reported having taken 11,000 prisoners.

Meanwhile, other elements of the 3ème DIA cleared the neighbouring hills of Germans surprised by the swift French advance and brought them down to Gémenos. (ECPAD)

Here in front of the town hall, prisoners were once made to tramp across a Nazi flag as they were marched off to a POW enclosure.

Konteradmiral Ruhfus, the place commander, surrendered on the morning of the 28th, together with 2,500 men on the Saint-Mandrier peninsula. He was taken on USS Catoctin but Vice Admiral Hewitt, on board the ship, did not take time to receive him. Ruhfus salutes as he leaves the ship with his chief of staff Fregattenkapitän Curt Rüling, on the first leg of their journey to a prison camp.
(US Navy, Naval History and Heritage Command)

Part One – Operation 'Dragoon' – The Invasion of Southern France • 139

The 7ème Régiment de Tirailleurs Algériens entered Marseille early on August 23 with elements of CC1 (1ère Division Blindée) following that evening. This Sherman of the 2ème Cuirassiers is advancing towards the city centre. (ECPAD)

More Shermans and an M8 armoured car, nicknamed Les Pyramides, line up in front of the Palais de Longchamp. (ECPAD)

The armour of CC1 soon reached the Cannebière, Marseille's main and famous thoroughfare. Here, another Sherman of the 2ème Cuirassiers covers the whole length of the street. This picture was taken at 7.30 p.m. on the 23rd while the Germans were still in control of most of the city. (ECPAD)

The church on the left is the Réformés.

The Germans held their ground and for three days the battle in Marseille became a matter of house to house fighting from street to street and from strong point to strong point with eager FFI support. From the corner of Boulevard Dugomier, men of the FFI fire across the Cannebière to the Grand Hôtel in which Germans have taken up position. (ECPAD)

No major changes have taken place in over 50 years in this corner of Marseille.

On August 26 in Marseille, Lieutenant Don Brinn, of the 163rd Signal Photo Company, pictured Lieutenant Edwin E. Dowell and a FFI watching the corner of a street in case a German soldier shows up. (USNA)

At the other corner of the block, men of the 3ème DIA set up a 57mm anti-tank gun ready to fire down the length of Boulevard Dugomier. Yet locals look on casually as if they were already watching a victory parade! (ECPAD)

The formal surrender became effective at 1 p.m. on the 28th when emissaries accompanied by a German went to Viste fort to arrange terms. With no indication as to the location, the author had not a little difficulty in tracing this particular street until a resident took him to Avenue Minerve, on the heights north of the city. (ECPAD)

Many changes have taken place here but the house visible on the left in the 1944 picture still remains, hidden by trees

The day of the final surrender, August 28, a crowd at Marseille sets fire to a German flag that had been flying over the prefecture of a police building. (USNA)

The first two weeks following the Allied landing in southern France exceeded all expectations as to the speed with which the objectives were taken. For the cost of 4,500 French and 2,700 American casualties, more than 57,000 prisoners had been taken and two major ports had been made available to Allied shipping a month ahead schedule. However, the direct effect of 'Dragoon' on 'Overlord' was virtually nil as Ob. West had already transferred all available forces from southern France to Normandy. Nevertheless, 'Dragoon' forced the withdrawal and scattering of all German forces from southern France, thus removing the threat of pressure against the long southern right flank of the US 12th Army Group advancing through northern France.

PART TWO: PURSUIT TO THE NORTH

THE BATTLE OF MONTÉLIMAR

General Truscott was dissatisfied with the arrangement for his control over CC1, which was due to serve initially as the VI Corps' reserve, so, anticipating an argument with de Lattre as to its employment, on August 1 he decided to organise a light mechanised combat command from his own forces. Under Brigadier General Frederick B. Butler, the VI Corps deputy commander, the brigade-sized task force included one battalion of the 143rd Infantry, two

Troops of the 3rd Division entered the city of Aix-en-Provence on August 21 to a 'cheerful greeting of the French' on Place de la Rotonde. (USNA)

More cheering civilians on August 22 in Place de la Rotonde to greet the 3rd Division. (USNA)

tank companies of the 753rd Tank Battalion, one company of the 636th Tank Destroyer Battalion, the 117th Cavalry Reconnaissance Squadron, the 59th Armored Field Artillery Battalion and a number of support units. Because of its late organisation, the force had not been loaded as a separate entity and its various elements could not be assembled inland before D + 2.

The 45th Division pressed on westwards and soon reached Pertuis, a major road junction 20 kilometres north of Aix-en-Provence. In the town main square, troops have a quick wash and brush up in the fountain. (USNA)

As in every town, motor cars are now master but the fountain in Place Jean Jaurès still runs.

Pursuit to the North **147**

Breakout from the Blue Line, August 17 - 19, a map from Riviera to the Rhine, the US Army Official History by Jeffrey J. Clarke and Robert Ross Smith.

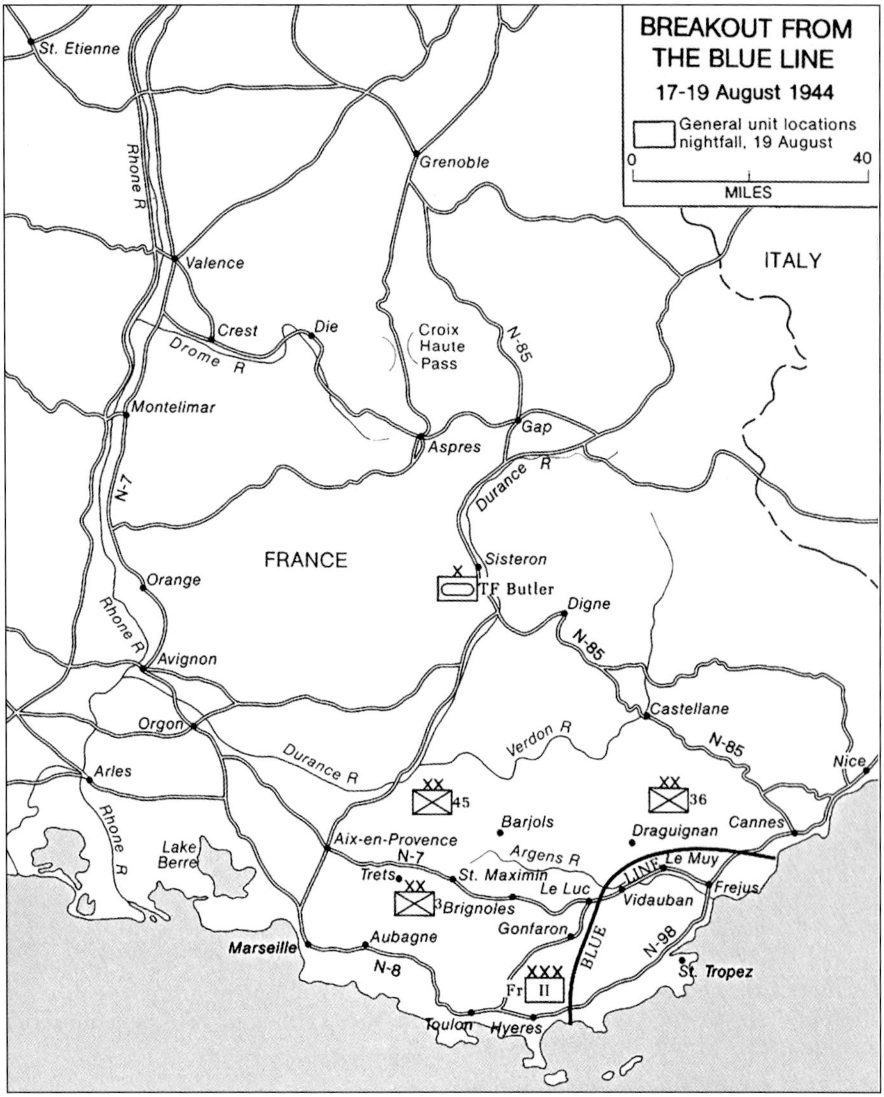

BREAKOUT FROM THE BLUE LINE
17-19 August 1944

General unit locations nightfall, 19 August

0 — 40 MILES

On August 28, T/5 Allan G. Smith, of the 163rd Signal Photo Company, pictured leaders of the 30th Infantry Regiment moving up with tank destroyers. The author had some difficulty finding where these photos had been taken: it was at Le Columbier, a hamlet 10 kilometres south-east of Montélimar. (USNA)

148 • OPERATION 'DRAGOON' AND BEYOND – THEN AND NOW

A M10 tank destroyer of the 601st Tank Destroyer Battalion 'nosing for the enemy, is poised for action as its crew scans the area for signs of German troops. Behind rises smoke from forest fire caused by shells.' (USNA)

Task Force Butler started out early on August 18 and by noon had reached the Verdon river north of Barjols. During the drive, at Draguignan, Troop C of the 117th Cavalry had bumped into elements of the LXII. Armeekorps that had escaped the airborne troops and captured the corps commander,

Original caption details that this half-track and 105mm gun were knocked-out by an anti-tank gun manned by T/4 Joseph Scroggins, Company C, 601st Tank Destroyer Battalion. He hits 'the first shot from about 3,000 yards'. (USNA)

General der Infanterie Ferdinand Neuling. However, all bridges in the area had been destroyed and, in spite of assistance by the FFI, the force was unable to get across the river before late afternoon. Then, with only four hours of daylight left, Butler decided to wait for the arrival of his supply column due to reach him that night.

Next morning, the task force resumed its advance with the bulk of the units having crossed to the west bank of the Durance to take advantage of better roads while two troops of cavalry advanced along the eastern bank. After a few skirmishes with isolated German elements, the cavalry entered Sisteron unopposed at about 6 p.m. The main column joined them some time later whereupon Butler re-assembled his force, refuelled his vehicles and waited for Truscott's orders to advance – either north to Grenoble or west to the Rhône valley. At noon, Patch had directed Truscott to alert one infantry division for a drive north to Grenoble and on the morning of August 20, the 36th Division started out to follow the trail of Task Force Butler.

Around noon on August 20, Truscott met Patch to request the latter's approval to send Task Force Butler west to the Rhône valley to block the German escape routes. Patch agreed but Truscott was then so worried by the uncertainty of the situation in the south that it was not before 8.45 p.m. that he radioed Butler, whose task force was still grouped in the Sisteron area, to move with all speed to Montélimar.

Riding on tank destroyers of the 645th TD Battalion, men of the 45th Infantry Division push on westward on August 18 but in the late afternoon they were to come up against stiff opposition at Tavernes and Barjols. (USNA)

The author found that this shot had been taken on the D560, three kilometres north-west of Salernes.

Early on the 18th, Task Force Butler started out northwards and by noon, the leading elements had reached the Verdon river. Here, a reconnaissance patrol of the 117th Cavalry Reconnaissance Squadron with Jeeps and M8 armoured cars ford the river beside the damaged bridge. (USNA)

The original caption said that this picture was taken 'in the Riez area' but the author had difficulty in finding this bridge until he discovered that it is now under 15 meters of water! Actually this spot, eight kilometres south of Moustiers-Sainte-Marie, was inundated when the Sainte-Croix dam was built in the early 1970s and the D957 now bypasses a large artificial lake.

The cables to the large suspension bridge over the Durance river near Mirabeau, 30 kilometres north-east of Aix-en-Provence, were severed but a footbridge was quickly built to span the gap and the 45th Division's engineers also soon established a pontoon bridge for vehicles further upstream. This picture was taken on the 20th. (USNA)

When the 11. Panzer-Division counter-attacked on the 25th, Kampfgruppe Thieme retook Grane, eight kilometres downstream of Crest. When the 11. Panzer-Division had to pull back on the 27th, they abandoned this PzKpfw III near Crest. A Diamond 6x6 wrecker of the 734th Ordnance Battalion recovered it for repair and further 'service with the French'. (USNA)

The skyline in the background enabled us to trace this field by the side of the D538, some three kilometres north of Crest.

By daybreak, Butler had regrouped and was proceeding westward without interference so that by late afternoon his vanguard had reached Crest, about 20 kilometres east of the Rhône, at which point they turned south to the Marsanne area. Taking FFI soldiers with them as infantry support, they probed toward La Coucourde and Sauzet, establishing road-blocks and posting Resistance men at key points. In the evening, tanks and tank destroyers opened up on the German convoys travelling on the highway down along the Rhône. Two artillery batteries, which had by then reached the Marsanne sector, unlimbered their pieces and added their fire. The threat to the Germans was obviously serious so next morning a Kampfgruppe advanced from Montélimar to deal with it. Forcing the American outpost and FFI back, it advanced as far as Sauzet and Puy. Follow-up elements of Task

On the 22nd, General Dahlquist was worried by his right flank so while he reorganised his scattered 36th Division, he sent the 143rd Infantry to Grenoble. In the afternoon, the French populace greet these men who were, according to the original caption, 'the first American troops to reach the town'. (USNA)

The picture was taken on the Rue Montorge.

Force Butler then reached Crest and counter-attacked, clearing Puy in the afternoon.

Meanwhile, the 36th Division had followed Task Force Butler and regrouped in the Sisteron area, but it was still not clear to Dahlquist, the division commander, whether he was to push north to Grenoble or west to Montélimar. Throughout August 21, Patch and Truscott still had their main interest in Toulon and Marseille and it was not before the late evening that Truscott finally ordered Dahlquist to move to Montélimar. Dahlquist spent the 22nd reorienting his scattered division and, worried by his right

On August 23, 1st Lt. Clarence E. Coggins was on a reconnaissance patrol with the leaders of the 45th Division arriving to Grenoble from the south when he came across a German patrol and was captured. He convinced the officer in charge that surrender was his only option and the German officer then freed him to return to friendly lines and arrange terms of surrender with his superiors. Terms were accepted, and so 942 enlisted men, 17 officers, and vast amounts of equipment were turned over to the 45th Division. This shot gives a nice view of the shoulder sleeve insignia of the 45th Division. The division's original shoulder insignia approved in 1924 featured a swastika, a common Native American symbol. With the rise of the Nazi in Germany, the division stopped using this insignia and a new one was approved in 1939 that featured the Thunderbird, another Native American symbol. Lt. Coggins was killed on January 4, 1945, in northern Alsace. (USNA)

flank, he allowed his 143rd Infantry to advance to Grenoble and enter the city in the afternoon.

Truscott arrived at the 36th Division's headquarters near Aspres about noon on the 22nd and voiced his dissatisfaction about the division's wide deployment and the fact that it was not yet attacking Montélimar. He wrote a note to Dahlquist, who was absent, insisting that 'the primary mission of the 36th Division is to block the Rhône valley in the gap immediately north of Montélimar'. To reassure Dahlquist about his right flank, Truscott gave him the 179th Infantry of the 45th Division for employment at Grenoble. Throughout the night and morning of the 23rd, greatly hampered by lack of fuel and transportation, Dahlquist and his staff strove to assemble and orient the forces under their command. Still uneasy,

The Germans had blown the Vercors Bridge over the Drac river. After the war, this bridge on Cours Berriat was rebuilt exactly as the original. (USNA)

Pursuit to the North **155**

On August 25 at Pont-de-Claix, five kilometres south of Grenoble, German prisoners were photographed as they marched southwards. The picture was taken from a window on the upper floor of the town hall but trees now completely hide the view. (USNA)

An agent of the town hall staff managed to call in a lorry with a hydraulic lift and position it right in front of the town hall to take this perfect comparison for us!

Truscott telephoned Dahlquist early on the 23rd to remind him that his task was to halt the German withdrawal up the Rhône valley. Yet, in spite of Truscott's pressure, Dahlquist displayed little energy that day in turning his forces north-east to the Montélimar battle area.

Having recognised the threat posed by the Americans above Montélimar, late on August 21 General Wiese had ordered his most-mobile force, the 11. Panzer-Division, to the threatened area. Fuel shortage, congestion on the roads, and marching at night under black-out conditions delayed the movement and the first sizeable elements did not reach Montélimar before noon on the 23rd. That day, though they sent small battlegroups through to Sauzet, the Germans were mainly occupied in sorting out the situation in Montélimar and organising their move northwards. A similar situation occurred on August 24 with the Germans urging their troops north and the Americans failing to counter the retreat. Expecting German attacks, Dahlquist was becoming increasingly concerned with defending the positions he already held instead of blocking the Rhône valley. On the afternoon of the 24th, he sent no less than four contradictory orders to the 143rd Infantry advancing to Valence until the regiment finally broke contact and headed back to Crest.

That evening, an American liaison officer in a Jeep came across a roadblock. As the Germans opened fire, he fled in haste leaving behind Dahlquist's

From the 26th, the Germans retreat northwards up the Rhône valley became more and more difficult. Artillery intermittently shelled the road and railway lines north of Montélimar, and Allied aircraft were an increasing nuisance. 'Road of ruin and retreat' is how the original caption described this scene on the N7 north of Montélimar. The remains of a 105mm horse-drawn battery 'caught by American fighter planes' had already been ransacked, first by the GIs and then by the local people. This view was taken looking north with the railway line in the left background. (USNA)

operational plans for the 25th. Now, with a clear picture of the American forces opposing them, Wiese decided to launch a strong counter-attack to clear the whole sector north-east of Montélimar. The 198. Infanterie-Division and several lesser units were put under Generalleutnant Wend von Wietersheim, the commander of the 11. Panzer-Division, who divided the forces under his control into six Kampfgruppen. With the intention of encircling and destroying the whole of the 36th Division, von Wietersheim planned an ambitious and complex operation with several co-ordinated and concentric attacks from south, west and north in the area between Montélimar and the Drôme river.

The operation started on the morning of August 25 but difficulties in communications and problems with deployment ruined the exceedingly demanding operation. Kampfgruppe Thieme retook Grane as planned but Kampfgruppe Wilde was late in reaching La Coucourde which was its objective and the sector was virtually unprotected when elements of the 141st Infantry moved out of the Condillac pass with the support of armour. By 7 p.m., two rifle companies, four tanks and seven tank destroyers were down in the valley, blocking the N7 highway. By midnight, von Wietersheim led a sharp charge against the road-block and within an hour, the Americans

August 28: 'This German convoy of approximately 400 vehicles was destroyed by cannon, mortar and small-arms fire on the outskirts of Montélimar'. (USNA)

The N7 has changed considerably and a precise comparison is difficult, but the hill in the distance enabled the author to pinpoint this length of the road near the southern entrance of Montélimar.

had been driven back into the Condillac pass. Three of the tanks and six of the TDs had been destroyed, yet Dahlquist had still committed little of his strength in the vital sector north of Montélimar.

On the 26th, the Germans renewed their efforts to clear the sector northeast of Montélimar, though less ambitiously than the previous day. In the south, their attack broke through a mile north of the Roubion river but two

Pursuit to the North 159

In 1943, the Germans had transferred to southern France Eisenbahn-Artillerie-Abteilung 640 with two batteries of railway guns: E-Art.Bttr. 692 with three 274mm and E-Art.Bttr. 698 with two 380mm guns. A third battery joined them early in 1944, E-Art.Bttr. 749 with two 280mm guns. From mid-August, Eisenbahn-Artillerie-Abteilung 640 pulled back northwards and, although one or two guns may have got through, most were blocked by wrecked trains just north of Montélimar. Stuck in between burnt-out carriages, these two 27,4cm Kanone (E) 592(f) of Eisenbahn-Artillerie-Batterie 692 appear to be undamaged. These photos were taken on September 1. (USNA)

American battalions, one each from the 142nd and 143rd Infantry, were pulled out of reserve and committed in a counter-attack and the situation was quickly restored. In the north, another Kampfgruppe came to within three kilometres of Crest but was too weak to press home the attack. Meanwhile, Task Force Butler had launched another attempt to cut the N7, two rifle companies attacking down the northern slope of Hill 300 while a platoon of tanks moved out of the Condillac pass to support them. The Germans reacted swiftly and the attack was halted, Dahlquist having failed again to commit enough of his force where it really counted.

Another of the heavies from Eisenbahn-Artillerie-Abteilung 640, a 38cm Siegfried Kanone from Eisenbahn-Artillerie-Batterie 698 abandoned at La Coucourde. (USNA)

On the far bank of the Rhône that flows behind the tree line, the mountain skyline permits a reasonably accurate comparison.

Hot pursuit! South of Montélimar, an M8 howitzer motor carriage (the M8 mounted a 75mm howitzer on an M5 light tank chassis) rolls up the N7 past the remains of a shattered German convoy. (USNA)

As for the Germans, the withdrawal was evolving successfully. Though American artillery intermittently shelled the road and railway lines along the Rhône, a steady stream of traffic continued throughout the day. East of the Rhône, the crossing of the Drôme proved to be a serious bottleneck since the Livron bridge had been badly damaged during the night of August 16/17 when an enterprising team from the FFI had blown a 20-metre section of the bridge. To the west, the bulk of the IV. Luftwaffen-Feldkorps had pulled abreast of Montélimar and continued retreating north. Controlling these movements was not easy and those elements of Flieger-Regiment 71 in the lead outdistanced the main body of the corps. They soon lost most of their vehicles to air attacks and FFI ambushes, many of the men joining up with the 11. Panzer-Division east of the river.

On the morning of the 26th, Truscott arrived at Dahlquist's headquarters, intending to relieve him of command. He started remonstrating with him for having failed to carry out his objective – to stop the German withdrawal – and complained that Dahlquist's situation reports had repeatedly proved to be wrong. In his defence, Dahlquist pointed out the shortages of fuel, ammunition and transportation and the renewed German attempts to break through his front. His resolve weakened, Truscott decided not to relieve Dahlquist for the moment, urging him instead to push Task Force Butler to the N7 at once and block it. Much to Truscott's disappointment, the renewed attack by a reinforced Task Force Butler on the 27th down the Condillac pass failed, and an attempt to drive northwards to Loriol on the 28th was equally unsuccessful.

Throughout the 27th and 28th, the Germans withdrew their troops northwards but their losses were mounting and the main road was now littered with dead horses and destroyed vehicles, while the railway line was blocked by wrecked trains, including heavy pieces of railway artillery. South of Montélimar, the 3rd Division overran a column of some 300 vehicles of the rearguard, taking 500 prisoners. During the night of August 28/29,

Grenadier-Regiment 326 succeeded in breaking through the La Coucourde gauntlet and withdrawing directly up the N7 but two other regiments of the 198. Infanterie-Division met the 143rd Infantry in the valley north of Sauzet, between Hills 300 and 430. They were broken up in the series of fire-fights and, though many of the grenadiers succeeded in reaching the N7, most were captured.

During the final battles on August 28-29, over 1,200 Germans were captured, including Generalmajor Otto Richter, the commander of the 198. Infanterie-Division. Clearing Montélimar, the 15th Infantry captured another 450 prisoners and 2,500 more were taken north-east of Montélimar when the sector was finally swept on the 30th.

The battle of southern France was over. In spite of heavy losses in personnel – some 20 per cent casualties to the units moving up the east bank of the Rhône (much less for the IV. Luftwaffen-Feldkorps west of the river) – and more losses in equipment, artillery and vehicles, the 19. Armee had managed to extract much of its forces from what might have been a deadly trap. Exhausted and disorganised, the army pulled back northwards, while the 11. Panzer-Division covered its flank against attacks from the east.

The official caption reads: 'An American wire man does his work under the wrecked sign of the town'. This was Le Logis-Neuf, 12 kilometres north of Montélimar. (USNA)

Two US Signal Corps photographers, Sergeant Leibowitz (left) and Sergeant Joseph P. Dieves (extreme right) and their driver, Private Raymond Rocha (second from left), captured these Germans in the woods north of Marsanne. (USNA)

We found that the picture was taken on Place Emile Loubet in Marsanne, not far from the town hall. Loriol is 20 kilometres north of Montélimar.

Signal Corps photo September 3, 'Junk of defeat'. The wreckage in the town of Loriol has been cleared from the road to make room for the 3rd Division pressing northwards. (USNA)

Official caption: 'Signal Corps photo, September 1. Happy welcome. Young and old of Valence greet entry of American troops into the town. Here four tank crewmen are welcomed, presented with a bottle of wine and asked many questions about the war and America.' (USNA)

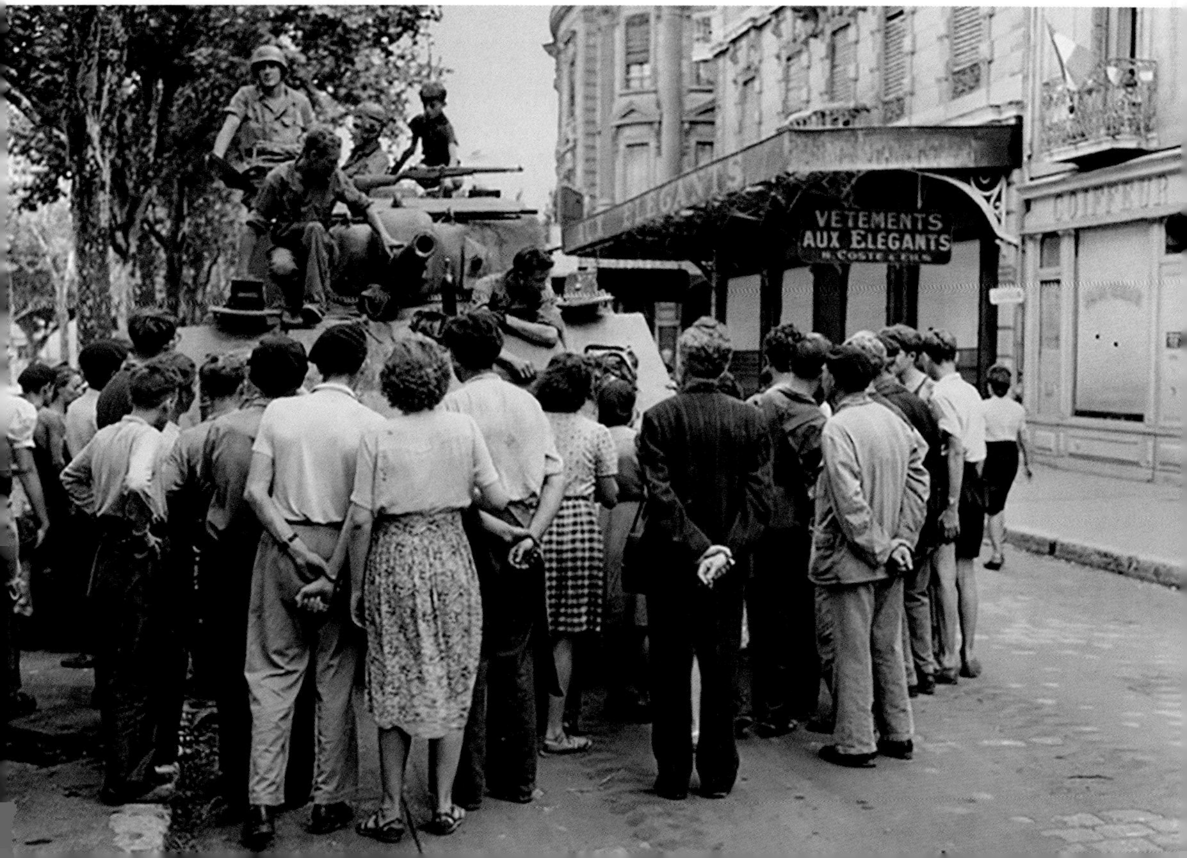

NORTH TO LYON

With the Germans in full retreat, and the vital ports of Toulon and Marseille secured, the next objective of the Seventh Army was to drive north to join with Eisenhower's forces advancing from Normandy. While the French completed the clearing of the harbours, from August 25 Patch began to send increasing supplies to the VI Corps to support the advance and on the 28th he issued new directives. The corps was to start out for Dijon as soon as possible with Lyon, the third largest city in France and an important road and rail centre, its immediate objective. West of the Rhône, the French were to push northwards in support. Truscott, who had directed the 45th Division to initiate reconnaissance northwards from Grenoble two days previously, speeded up the move. He ordered the 36th Division to advance along the east bank of the Rhône to Lyon and the 45th Division to move to Bourg-en-Bresse, 60 kilometres north-east of the city. The 3rd Division was to follow the 45th Division, ready to support either division if necessary.

Concerned with the possibility of an Allied attempt at a wide envelopment north of Lyon, the Germans continued to retreat northwards. Wiese assigned the IV. Luftwaffen-Feldkorps the mission of holding Lyon, where the FFI had started a major uprising, and controlling the traffic through it. He planned to pull his rearguards out of the city on the night of September 2/3, after all bridges across the Rhône and Saône rivers had been blown. Warned about the Americans outflanking his withdrawing forces from the east, he ordered the 11. Panzer-Division to secure the Rhône and Ain river bridges east of Lyon before the enemy reached the area, but it was too late. On August 29, having encountered only weak opposition, the 45th Division had captured two bridges over the Rhône and during the next few days, advanced further north to Meximieux, about 30 kilometres north-east of Lyon, and to Pont-d'Ain on the Ain river. Having failed to secure the crossings before the Americans reached them, Wiese now ordered the 11. Panzer-Division to try to disrupt the American advance. Isolated engagements ensued on September 1, the most serious being at Meximieux where a small infantry/tank Kampfgruppe cut through the rear of the two leading regiments of the 45th Division. However, as American units returned to the town from the north, the Germans started pulling back. Fighting to clear the Meximieux area continued throughout the night, losses being over 100 German and some 200 American, most of them being taken prisoner.

On September 1, with Patch's consent, Truscott decided to leave the honour of formally entering Lyon to French troops and directed the 36th Division to bypass the city to the east. Also, he pressed Dahlquist to launch a major attack towards Bourg-en-Bresse the following day.

On September 2, when the 45th Division's two leading regiments tried to reach Bourg-en-Bresse as ordered, they found that the Germans now presented a fairly strong coherent front. Hoping to find weak points in the German defences, Truscott ordered the 117th Cavalry Squadron to send

When the 45th Division reached the Rhône on August 29, General der Infanterie Wiese ordered the 11. Panzer-Division to disrupt their advance. On September 1, at Meximieux, 30 kilometres north-east of Lyon, a small Kampfgruppe cut through the rear of the leading American regiments and at dusk units of the 179th and 157th Infantry were sent back to Meximieux from the north. With their line of retreat threatened, the Germans finally broke off the action but the Americans were unable to recover the area until the early hours of September 2. Matériel losses to the 179th Infantry and supporting units during the Meximieux affair amounted to seven vehicles destroyed, including two tank destroyers and two armoured cars. The Germans had lost a dozen tanks in and around the town, one of them being this Panther lying on Place Vaugelas but as so often happened the original caption promoted it to the rank of a 'Tiger'. (USNA)

The Lion d'Or Hôtel is still in business today under the same name.

Pursuit to the North **167**

On September 3, elements of the 117th Cavalry Squadron (Troop B plus one platoon of Troop A) were trapped in Montrevel by elements of the 11. Panzer-Division. They had to surrender that evening and lost all their vehicles, about 40 armoured cars and Jeeps, together with over 150 men, mostly POWs. This M5 light tank was disabled on the D975, at the northern entrance of the village.

Fifty-five years later Montrevel remains almost timeless.

Meanwhile, the 19. Armee pushed its exhausted and disorganised forces northwards. In Lyon, an unknown French photographer took, discreetly, these pictures of the last German troops in town.

out recce patrols. Elements of the cavalry were able to slip through and two troops reached Montrevel, a village on the N75, the main road northwest from Bourg, only to find themselves trapped there by elements of the 11. Panzer-Division. A counter-attack to relieve them was made on the afternoon of September 3 but to no avail and the surrounded cavalrymen had to surrender that evening. Troop B and one platoon of Troop A had lost

In the Rue de la République, he snatched a shot of a 37mm AA gun (SdKfz 161/3 in German parlance) of the 11. Panzer-Division.

The Germans finally evacuated Lyon during the night of September 2/3, after all bridges across the Rhône and Saône rivers had been blown. This Panther tank of the 11. Panzer-Division was pictured at the eastern end of the La Guillotière bridge.

A new roundabout has now replaced the tree-lined square.

The trek northwards continues. We are now at Villefranche-sur-Saône, 30 kilometres north of Lyon, where a convoy shelters in the shade on the Rue Nationale.
(Bundesarchiv)

This was then the main street running through the city.

On September 3, French forces and elements of the 36th Divisions entered Lyon and found that the city had been abandoned by the Germans. The situation was hopeless but the Miliciens decided to fight on to the end. Soldiers take cover behind the parapet while shots are fired at snipers hidden in the Hôtel Dieu hospital. In right background, the Wilson Bridge. (USNA)

'Allied troops receive gala welcome upon entering Lyon' noted the original caption. Joyful over the absence of Germans in their city, people of all ages shake hands with these troops of the 36th Division. (USNA)

all their vehicles – about 40 armoured cars and Jeeps – together with over 150 men, mostly captured. Lieutenant Daniel W. Lee, commanding Headquarters Platoon, Troop A, was awarded the Medal of Honor for gallantry in action at Montrevel in spite of severe wounds. Though Truscott later charged the 117th Cavalry with carelessness, as official US Army historians Jeffrey J. Clarke and Robert Ross Smith point out in Riviera to the Rhine, 'it is hard to escape the conclusion that Truscott simply assigned missions to the 117th Cavalry that were beyond its capabilities'.

The Germans evacuated Lyon during the night of September 2/3 and the following afternoon, the main body of the 19. Armee was north of Macon. That day, September 3, French forces entered Lyon and found the city totally evacuated. Bypassing the city to the west, CC2 of the 1ère Division Blindée pushed northwards and succeeded in trapping the rearguard of the IV. Luftwaffen-Feldkorps some 30 kilometres north of Lyon, taking nearly 2,000

A US Signal Corps photographer took this picture of 'a Milicien who had taken up arms against the FFI and Allies' being led away by FFI. (USNA)

The author discovered that the picture had been taken on Place Gabriel Péri.

Encountering no opposition, the 45th Division entered Bourg-en-Bresse on the morning of September 4. By 10 a.m., sniper fire was reported cleared and troops made their way into the city proper. Here, an M10 tank destroyer of the 645th TD Battalion rolls into the town via the N75. (USNA)

Boulevard du Brou, over half a century later.

prisoners as a result. On the morning of the 4th, VI Corps found that the bulk of the German forces facing them had once again escaped. Encountering no opposition, the 45th Division entered Bourg-en-Bresse, while the leading units of the 36th Division moved into Macon. On the right wing, the 3ème DIA was moving abreast of the VI Corps, probing the Jura mountains along the Swiss border.

Pursuit to the North **175**

Further down Boulevard du Brou, the people of Bourg-en-Bresse stood and cheered as troops of the 157th Infantry, 45th Division, marched through their town on September 4. The 141st Infantry regimental historian later recalled what he dubbed the 'Champagne Campaign': 'For three days our columns rumbled north, giving birth to impressions that will always remain with us: mountains and fertile green valleys; little villages with huge cathedrals; the bells in every little village announcing the liberation as the first doughboy-laden tank grinds through the cheering crowds; steel helmets filled with eggs; cakes of rich butter rolled in clean wet leaves; a peasant woman with her apron filled with not quite ripened apples...' (USNA)

THE DIJON SALIENT

Patch's original plans had called for the VI Corps to drive north on the left wing to join with the Third Army advancing from the west while, on the right, the French forces were to head north-east for the Belfort gap, the Alsace and the Rhine. On September 2, in view of the current deployment of forces, Truscott suggested a change in plan as the French were in a better position to pursue the retreating Germans northwards leaving his own forces to advance to the Belfort gap. Patch agreed on the morning of the 3rd but de Lattre at first did not as he felt that, with his forces split

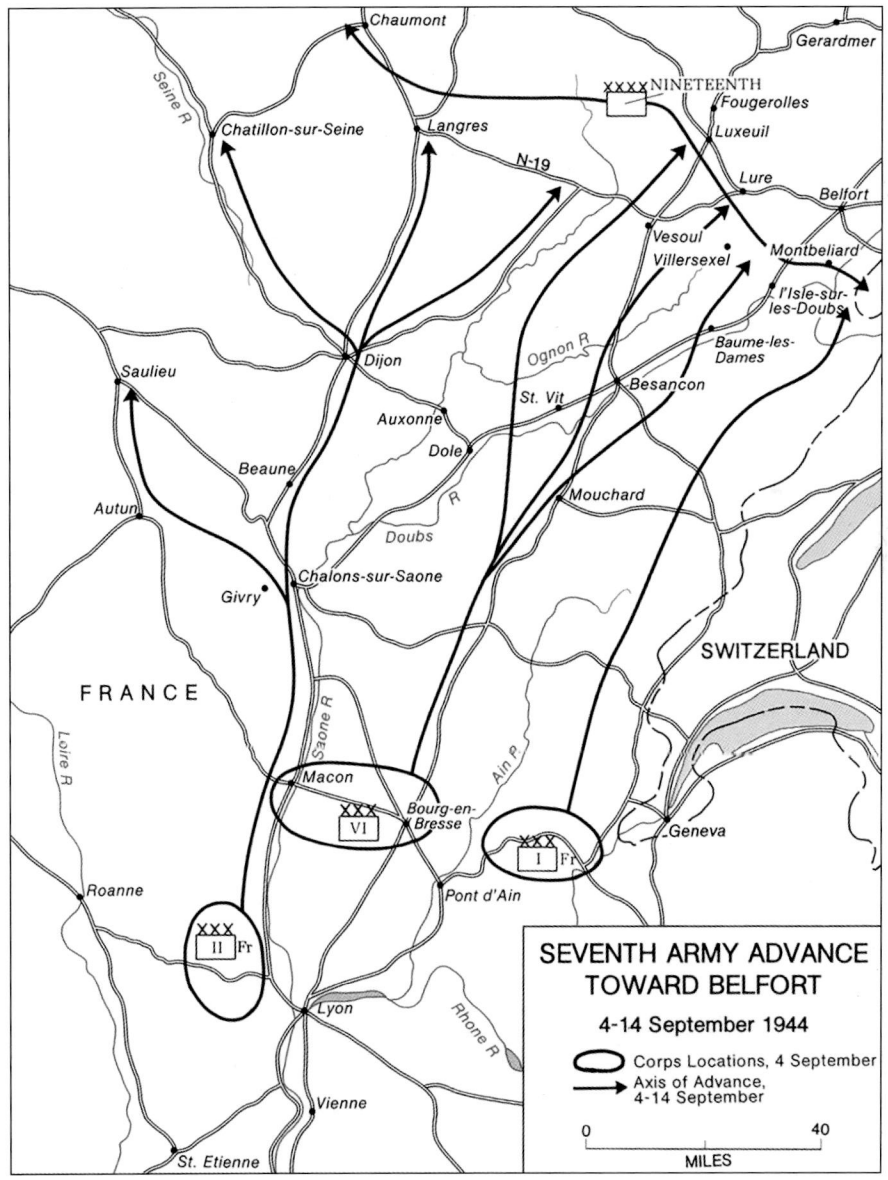

On the Seventh Army's right wing, the VI Corps pressed northwards on September 4 with the 3rd Division in the lead, the 36th Division on the left and the 45th Division in the rear. A map from Riviera to the Rhine, the US Army Official History by Jeffrey J. Clarke and Robert Ross Smith.

Pursuit to the North **177**

The leading elements of the 3rd Division approached Besançon on September 5 and quickly moved to surround the area before the German defenders could react. On the 6th, these soldiers of the 7th Infantry were pictured in Larnod, getting ready to attack German positions in the Avanne area. (USNA)

on both sides of VI Corps, it would be difficult, if not impossible, to unify them as an independent French army sometime in the near future. In the end he compromised and accepted Truscott's proposal but announced the formation of two French corps headquarters: the IIème Corps d'Armée to control the forces pushing north along the Rhône and Saône rivers and the Ier Corps d'Armée to operate on the right of the VI Corps. Not wishing to make an issue, Patch agreed and issued the appropriate orders on the 4th.

This same day, the 7th Infantry crossed the Doubs river into Avanne, which was quickly liberated. (USNA)

Two days of fighting followed before Besançon fell late on the 8th, half the defending troops having been killed or captured. A Signal Corps photographer took this shot of infantrymen of A Company, 30th Infantry Regiment crossing a walkway above the Doubs River at Besancon. (USNA)

On a street where there was once a gaping hole crossed by a Bailey bridge... this is the rather disappointing comparison of the Battant bridge in Besançon.

'A long convoy of tanks move up to the front'. These were Sherman tanks from the 191st Tank Battalion attached to the 45th Division. (USNA)

This picture was taken on the D942, just a kilometre from Ornans which lies 25 kilometres south of Besançon. The armour is moving northwards in the direction of Baume-les-Dames. (USNA)

By September 5, after a further withdrawal, Armeegruppe G was extended along a wide front centred on Dijon. Held by the ragged elements of the LXXXV. Armeekorps and IV. Luftwaffen-Feldkorps backed by the 11. Panzer-Division, the eastern end of this salient rested on the Swiss border near Pontarlier. From Chalon to Langres, the western sector of the front was rather a bridgehead west of Dijon, held open while the forces retreating from the Atlantic coast under LXIV. Armeekorps moved through it. Blaskowitz's main concern was with his right flank, thinly-held by LXVI. Armeekorps with an assortment of forces, mostly security and service units of all types just scraped together. Elements of the

From the window of a house in Genlis, 15 kilometres east of Dijon, a photographer surreptitiously took pictures of the German withdrawal, these shots showing a long column of horse-drawn carts, followed by some camouflaged vehicles. (ECPAD)

Pursuit to the North

Some hours later, from the same window, he photographed the sudden arrival of the tanks of the 1ère Division Blindée. (ECPAD)

This particular house has been demolished since but the author took this near-comparison from the first floor of the Hôtel du Commerce which still stands at the end of what is now the Avenue du Général de Gaulle.

Another picture of the 'Champagne Campaign' as an M5 of the 1ère Division Blindée crosses Place Darcy in Dijon on September 11. As the 141st Infantry regimental history summed up: 'Rich red wine from the Rhône; a little girl with a French flag throwing a clumsily made corsage tied together with a bit of red, white and blue ribbon that stings your face as you roll on northward; a group of mountaineers with FFI brassards on their arms and nondescript fire-arms resting easily in the crooks of their arms, standing beside a bridge that is standing untouched waiting for American tanks to rumble across it and onward towards Germany... Vive La France! Vive L'Amérique! This was the way to fight a war!' (USNA)

16. Infanterie-Division arriving from the Atlantic were quickly rushed to LXVI. Armeekorps and ordered to deploy north and north-west of Langres, 60 kilometres north of Dijon. On the right flank, the tactical link with the 1. Armee, which had been totally lost since August 26, was weakly re-established on the 4th.

Between September 4 and 8, Seventh Army's advance northwards continued, encountering only disorganised resistance. On the left, the IIème Corps d'Armée cleared Chalon on the 5th, but stopped on the 6th to wait for fuel to resume its drive. They reached the Beaune area on the 7th where they came across groups from the LXIV. Armeekorps trying to reach Dijon. On September 7 and 8, the French rounded up around 1,000 men of the 16. Infanterie-Division and 159. Reserve-Division and six railway trains, one of them armoured, packed with troops, guns and supplies. On the army's right wing, the VI Corps also pressed northwards on September 4, heading for Besançon, with the 3rd Division in the lead, the 36th Division on the left and the 45th Division in the rear. On the corps right flank, the 3ème DIA was moving abreast. After two days of desultory fighting, Besançon fell to the 3rd Division late on the 8th.

Pursuit to the North **183**

On September 16, shortly after the liberation of Lure, James A. Cuca pictured civilians crowding around soldiers of the 3rd Division. By then, the character of the fighting changed from the pursuit operation to a grinding advance against firm German resistance. (USNA)

That same day, with all the units withdrawing from the Atlantic coast having joined up, Blaskowitz ordered another major withdrawal. On its left wing, the 19. Armee pulled back from the Doubs river and established a new defensive line centred around Vesoul. In the centre, the LXIV. Armeekorps fell back swiftly, abandoning Dijon, while on the right the LXVI. Armeekorps withdrew to the axis of Langres–Chaumont which swung north-eastwards to join with 1. Armee near Bayon, just south of Nancy. Also on the 8th, Ob. West transferred control of the 1. Armee, formerly on Heeresgruppe B's southern wing, to Armeegruppe G.

Dijon fell without a fight to the French on September 11. They pushed north-west beyond the city and the union of the 'Overlord' and 'Dragoon' armies was achieved that day when elements of the French 2ème Dragons met a patrol from the US 6th Armored Division at Saulieu.

For both sides, one major campaign had ended and a new one was about to begin. Though Armeegruppe G had succeeded to extricate a substantial part of its forces from western and southern France, the losses had been heavy. Between September 3 and 14, Seventh Army had captured over 12,000 prisoners, about half taken by the Americans and half by the French, which brought the total number of prisoners since August 15 to over 45,000. To this figure must be added the 31,000 men taken by the French at Toulon and Marseilles, the 24,000 or so hopelessly isolated in the fortresses on the Atlantic coast and the 20,000 men of Gruppe Elster, now cut off south of the Loire. All in all, the grand total came to around 40 per cent of the original strength of Armeegruppe G on August 15.

It was the end of the 'Champagne Campaign'. T/5 Allan G. Smith pictured troops of Company C, 7th Infantry, 3rd Division, advancing northwards in the rain through Rupt-sur-Moselle. (USNA)

'Dragoon' meets 'Overlord'! On September 15, this picture made the headline in the Stars and Stripes: 'Here is the first picture of the meeting of American troops of the Third US Army with French troops of the Seventh Army'. Dragon Jean Quignon shakes hands with Corporal Carl Newman. On the left stands Champs Elysées, an M8 of the 2ème Dragons, Seventh Army, crewed by Adjudant Emile Lancery, Dragon Emile Lalanne and Dragon Quignon, while on the right stands Butch, an M8 of the 86th Cavalry Reconnaissance Squadron, Third Army, with Sergeant Louis Basil, Corporal Edgar Ellis and Corporal Newman. (USNA)

The historic meeting took place in front of the town hall in Autun.

In a second picture, Adjudant Lancery shakes hands with Sergeant Basil while Lieutenant Vernon Hill looks on. Actually, these pictures were taken on September 13, three days after the real first meetings between the 'Dragoon' and 'Overlord' forces. As with other link-ups, the time and place of the first contact between Seventh Army and Third Army is still a subject of controversy. Individuals in single Jeeps may well have established early contact with patrols of the other army and recce elements of both forces had already met near Sombernon in the late evening of the 10th. Also, at least one courier plane of the 2ème Division Blindée landed near the same town the following afternoon. The Supreme Allied Commander Mediterranean gave September 11 as the date of the first meeting while the French accepted September 12. As to the link-up at Autun which had made the headline in the Stars and Stripes, the author managed to trace four of the men involved – two Americans and two Frenchmen – and one of them, Jean Quignon, explained precisely what happened. Flanking the advance of the IIème Corps d'Armée, the 2ème Dragons had reached the town on the night of September 8/9. Skirmishes took place throughout the 9th but the French pushed northwards and on the 10th reached Saulieu and Sombernon, west of Dijon. As the situation at Autun was still unclear, a squadron of the 2ème Dragons was sent back to secure the town. On the 11th, the situation progressively improved and late in the afternoon, a patrol from the 2ème Dragons met a unit from the 6th Armored Division, US Third Army, at Saulieu. The next day, elements of the Third Army arrived at Autun. The 2ème Dragons' squadron was still in the town on September 13 when orders arrived from higher up: the Americans wanted to take pictures of the link-up between Seventh Army and Third Army and an armoured car had to be sent 'to make the junction in front of the town hall'. Champs Elysées was ordered to the town hall where an American M8 was waiting and the 'meeting' pictures were taken. On September 15, Stars and Stripes put the picture on its front page and gave the names of the men involved as well as their home towns. (USNA)

PART THREE: THE BATTLE OF ALSACE

SHAEF'S STRATEGY

On September 15 General Eisenhower, the Supreme Commander of the Allied forces in northern France, assumed operational control of the forces in southern France too. At the same time Headquarters of the US 6th Army Group, under Lieutenant General Devers, became operational in southern France taking command of the US Seventh Army and the French 1ère Armée.

Eisenhower would have preferred transferring the Seventh Army to General Bradley's 12th Army Group but that would have reduced the American contingent within 6th Army Group to just a few units: the 1st Airborne Task Force (guarding the Franco-Italian border in the south), some artillery at the front and logistical units along the line of communications to the Mediterranean. In such a situation, with the army group reduced mainly to the 1ère Armée, the French would logically have pressed for French command of it. So, not wishing to have to deal personally with French national interests, Eisenhower had no choice but to keep a sizeable American contingent in the 6th Army Group.

However, the Supreme Commander really had no role to assign to the 6th Army Group. SHAEF's existing plans called for a drive into Germany by only two army formations, one operating north of the Ardennes forest (Field Marshal Bernard L. Montgomery's British 21st Army Group and most of the US First Army of Bradley's 12th Army Group) and the other (the right wing of US First Army) to the south. The US Third Army (on 12th Army Group's right wing) was relegated to a secondary role, its eastward advance limited to securing bridgeheads over the Moselle river. As to the 6th Army Group, Eisenhower expected little from it, convinced as he was that even the most successful advances in the south had little strategic potential. Devers' army group faced large expanses of terrain highly favourable to the defence – the Vosges mountains, the Rhine river and the Black Forest – and even if his Franco-American forces were somehow able to push through these barriers, the capture of Nuremberg or Munich did not seem especially worthwhile objectives.

As pointed out by Jeffrey J. Clarke and Robert Ross Smith in Riviera to the Rhine, the US Army's official history dealing with 6th Army Group's operations in France, there were alternatives that neither Eisenhower nor

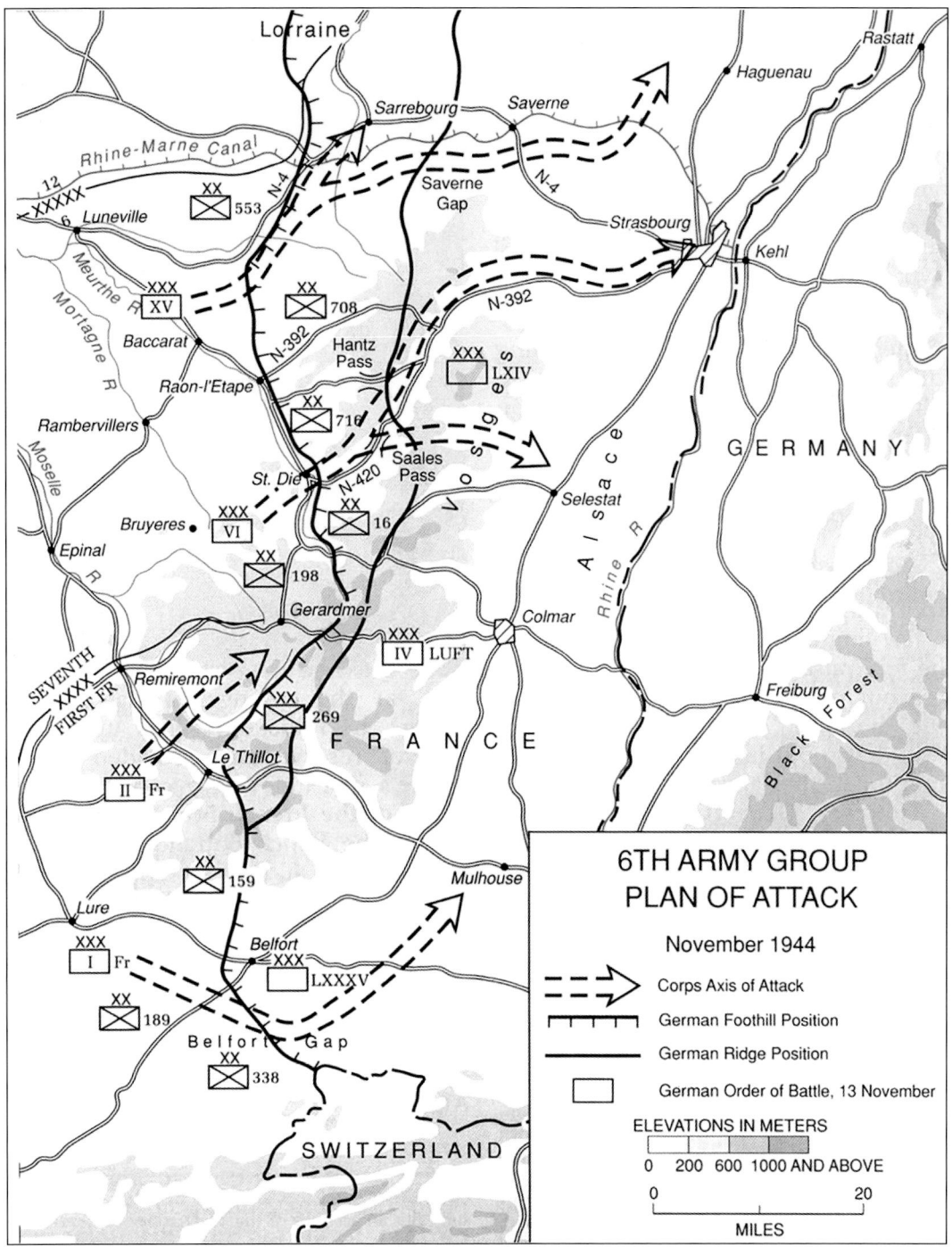

The directive did not specify a date for the 6th Army Group supporting offensive. Devers set November 15 as his target date and he drew up plans to launch the Seventh Army and the 1ère Armée in a series of attacks. On the right, the 1ère Armée was to breach the Belfort gap. On the left, the Seventh Army was to head northwards, with, on its left wing, the XV Corps aiming for Sarrebourg to then swing east and force the Saverne gap. On the army's right wing, the VI Corps was to advance through the Vosges mountains to break out onto the Alsatian plains and then to seize Strasbourg. A map from Riviera to the Rhine, the US Army Official History by Jeffrey J. Clarke and Robert Ross Smith.

In mid-October, the VI Corps launched an attack aiming at Saint-Dié, one of the cornerstones of the German defence positions at the foot of the western Vosges. On the 14th, T/4 Arland Musser of the 163rd Signal Photo Company pictured men of Company I, 143rd Regiment, 36th Division, moving down a road leading to Fays. In his original caption he noted that they were going to 'set up and mortar the nearby town held by the Germans.' (USNA)

his SHAEF planners ever considered, namely to send 'a reinforced 6th Army Group north through the Rhenish plains in a vast enveloping manoeuvre against the flank or rear of the German forces defending the Saar and Ruhr regions; or sending it north as far as Frankfurt and then north-east, following the famous Napoleonic route toward Berlin through the critical Fulda corridor.'

Not yet aware of Eisenhower's indifference to their efforts, Devers and his staff drew up plans to cross the Rhine near Rastatt, 50 kilometres north of Strasbourg, from where they would gain good routes leading east and north-east into Germany or, alternatively, north up the Rhine valley to Karlsruhe and Mannheim.

Eisenhower did not object to these plans. As put by Clarke and Smith: 'Possibly SHAEF approved 6th Army Group's offensives toward Strasbourg and the Rhine only because they did not appear to interfere in any way with the northern effort; furthermore, Eisenhower must have hoped that the southern army group's separate line of communications might enable him to increase the 12th Army Group's logistical support at some future date

On November 4, the 3rd Division broke through Le Haut Jacques pass, ten kilometres west of Saint-Dié. (USNA)

The author traced that this Sherman of the 756th Tank Battalion had bogged down at Les Rouges-Eaux, a few kilometres before reaching Le Haut Jacques pass.

As the VI Corps pressed for Saint-Dié, the French IIème Corps d'Armée launched a supporting attack in the south on November 3. This picture was taken the following day when elements of the 3ème Division d'Infanterie Algérienne captured Rochesson, 30 kilometres south of Saint-Dié and the key to another road leading to the Vosges high passes. (USNA)

Our comparison was taken in front of the village town hall.

US Army photographer, Sergeant Leibowitz, pictured this signals team of the 3ème Division d'Infanterie Algérienne using a mule to bring wire up the mountain road at Rochesson on November 4. (USNA)

once the capacity of the Mediterranean supply system had been sufficiently expanded. But as long as Devers remained logistically independent, Eisenhower was apparently willing to give him a certain freedom of action.'

On September 22, Eisenhower met with his subordinate commanders, including Devers and Patch, to consider new plans. The conference specified that the 6th Army Group, with its separate line of communication north of the Mediterranean, could continue its offensive towards Strasbourg as well as its efforts to cross the Belfort gap. Devers reiterated his request for another corps for the Seventh Army and he asked that the two-division XV Corps of the Third Army, which operated just north of the 6th Army Group, be assigned to him. Noting that his army group could easily support both XV Corps and at least one additional division, over his existing line of communication from the south, Devers pointed out that such a transfer of logistical responsibility would greatly alleviate the burden of the 12th Army Group supply system.

As pointed out by Clarke and Smith: 'At the time, Devers' proposals were especially appealing to the harried SHAEF tactical and logistical planners' and on September 26 Eisenhower decided to transfer the XV Corps to the 6th Army Group. He also decided that three American divisions, which had been scheduled to join the 12th Army Group after landing in northern France, should be diverted to Marseille for the 6th Army Group.

On September 29, control of the XV Corps officially passed to the 6th

On the VI Corps' northern wing the US 100th Division started south-eastwards through a forested area on November 12. It was the first time the 'Century' Division was going into combat. Hindered by rain and muddy mountain trails, on the 16th the GIs finally reached the crest of a hill from where they overlooked the Plaine river valley, in the rear of the German defences at Raon-l'Étape. These men of the division's 398th Regiment were pictured on November 17 when the American attackers started to pour down the hills. By November 18, Raon-l'Étape was clear of German troops. (USNA)

Army Group and Seventh Army. The main elements of the corps were the 79th Infantry Division, the French 2ème Division Blindée; and the 106th Cavalry Group, consisting of the 106th and 121st Cavalry Squadrons and the 813th Tank Destroyer Battalion.

On October 18 at Brussels, Eisenhower, Montgomery and Bradley worked out plans for the November operations of the 21st and 12th Army Groups, and on the 28th Eisenhower issued his Directive No. 114 promulgating his orders for operations in November and December. It confirmed that the main Allied effort would be borne by the 21st Army Group and the left wing of the 12th Army Group. In the centre, the right wing of the US First Army and the US Third Army were to seize the Saar basin, advance north-eastwards to the Rhine and secure bridgeheads opposite the Frankfurt area. Timed to support the main effort north of the Ardennes, these operations were

Meanwhile, on the 6th Army Group right wing, the 1ère Armée was to breach the Belfort gap. This Signal Corps photo shows French troops crossing the Doubs river at Pont-de-Roide, 30 kilometres south of Belfort. (USNA)

The Germans had blown the bridge over the Doubs when they continued their withdrawal northwards. The small footbridge had been built a few hundred metres downstream from the ruined span.

The Battle of Alsace

clearly subsidiary. The directive confirmed Eisenhower's indifference to the 6th Army Group potential and Devers was told to protect the right flank of the 12th Army Group, clearing the sector west of the Rhine and ultimately establishing bridgeheads in the vicinity of Karlsruhe and Mannheim.

The directive set no firm timetable but it soon turned out that Eisenhower expected the left wing of 12th Army Group to start the offensive sometime between November 1 and 5 with the 21st Army Group to follow about November 10. The Third Army was to launch its attack against the Saar as soon as its logistical situation permitted, but not later than five days after 12th Army Group had jumped off. The directive did not specify a date for the 6th Army Group supporting offensive but, after consulting with General Bradley and General Patton of the Third Army, General Patch of the Seventh Army, and Général de Lattre of the 1ère Armée, Devers set November 15 as his own target date.

Devers planned to launch both the Seventh Army and the 1ère Armée in a series of attacks. On the Seventh Army's left, the US XV Corps was to start on D-Day, November 15, heading north-eastward for Sarrebourg. The corps was then to swing east and force the Saverne gap. On the army's right wing, the US VI Corps would follow on D+2, advancing through the Vosges mountains to break out onto the Alsatian plains. The corps was then to seize Strasbourg and secure the west bank of the Rhine north and south of the city.

In the sector of the 1ère Armée, further south, the Ier Corps d'Armée, located on the right wing along the Swiss border, was to launch the army's main effort on or about November 15, its task being to breach the Belfort gap. On the army's left wing, the IIème Corps d'Armée was to launch a subsidiary attack in the Vosges sometime between November 10 and 15, both to support the American VI Corps on its left and to divert German attention away from the Belfort gap.

Tactical developments and poor flying conditions soon forced a change in plans and on November 2 Eisenhower and Bradley decided to postpone the First Army attacks to the 10th. Hoping to have at least some of his forces attacking earlier, however, Bradley asked Patton to have his Third Army begin its offensive as soon as possible and have his XII Corps, just north of the Seventh Army, attack no later than November 8. Devers visited Patton's command post at Nancy on November 5 but he was apparently not informed of the decisions taken and returned from the briefing with the understanding that Third Army's attack was still scheduled for the 10th.

Consequently, the 6th Army Group headquarters was surprised when word came on November 7 that Third Army's XII Corps would begin its attack on the morning of the 8th. Devers quickly decided to move his starting date forward to November 13 and new orders were immediately sent to General Patch of the Seventh Army and Général de Lattre of the 1ère Armée. The XV Corps and both the French corps were now to attack on the 13th; the VI Corps was to follow on the 15th.

Devers was optimistic. He estimated that the Ier Corps d'Armée would be in the Rhine valley by December 1 and that the XV Corps would have crossed the Vosges and broken out onto the Alsatian plains by the same date. As Clarke and Smith commented: 'Devers' own prediction was for crossing the Rhine above Strasbourg and exploiting north up the Rhine valley toward Karlsruhe, thus trapping the German 1. Armee and isolating the Saar industrial region in one sweep. This time he would show the other Allied commanders what his underrated forces could do.'

GERMAN PLANS AND DEPLOYMENT

By mid-November, 6th Army Group's front coincided with that of the German 19. Armee, for Heeresgruppe G, to which the latter belonged, had just extended the army sector northward to the Rhine-Marne Canal which also marked the boundary between the Allied 6th and 12th Army Groups.

After the hectic withdrawal from southern France in the summer, 19. Armee's lines were stretched to breaking point but the difficult terrain in the Vosges had slowed the Allied advance in the last weeks and saved the army from collapse. To make things worse General Wiese, the army commander, could not count on any reinforcement, for his sector had a low priority on the western front. At Ob. West, Generalfeldmarschall Gerd von Rundstedt's major concern was to counter the expected Allied drive against the Ruhr and he accordingly gave priority to Heeresgruppe B which defended that sector. Also, von Rundstedt was striving to assemble forces for the Ardennes counter-offensive scheduled for late November and to this end he had already moved several armoured units from Heeresgruppe G to Heeresgruppe B. Finally, General der Panzertruppen Hermann Balck, the Heeresgruppe G commander, had to give priority to his 1. Armee which was defending the Saar region. The 21. Panzer-Division would soon be taken away from 19. Armee and diverted north of the Rhine-Marne Canal to join the 1. Armee and Panzerbrigade 106, Heeresgruppe G's only significant reserve, followed likewise. Thus, the only armour left to Wiese were some assault gun units.

On the 19. Armee's right wing, the LXIV. Armeekorps had in the line, from north to south, the 553. Volksgrenadier-Division, made up of only two regiments; Grenadier-Regiment 951; the weak 21. Panzer-Division; the battered 716. Infanterie-Division and what was left of the badly damaged 16. Volksgrenadier-Division. On November 8, the 708. Volksgrenadier-Division began moving into the lines on the left of the 553. Volksgrenadier-Division, first relieving Grenadier-Regiment 951 and then taking over from the 21. Panzer-Division. LXIV. Armeekorps faced the Seventh Army's XV Corps and most of the VI Corps.

In the army's centre, the IV. Luftwaffen-Feldkorps defended the southern section of the Vosges below Saint-Dié with two divisions: the understrength but experienced 198. Infanterie-Division, most of which confronted the VI Corps' southern wing; and the fairly good 269. Infanterie-Division, recently arrived from Norway, which faced the northern wing of IIème Corps d'Armée.

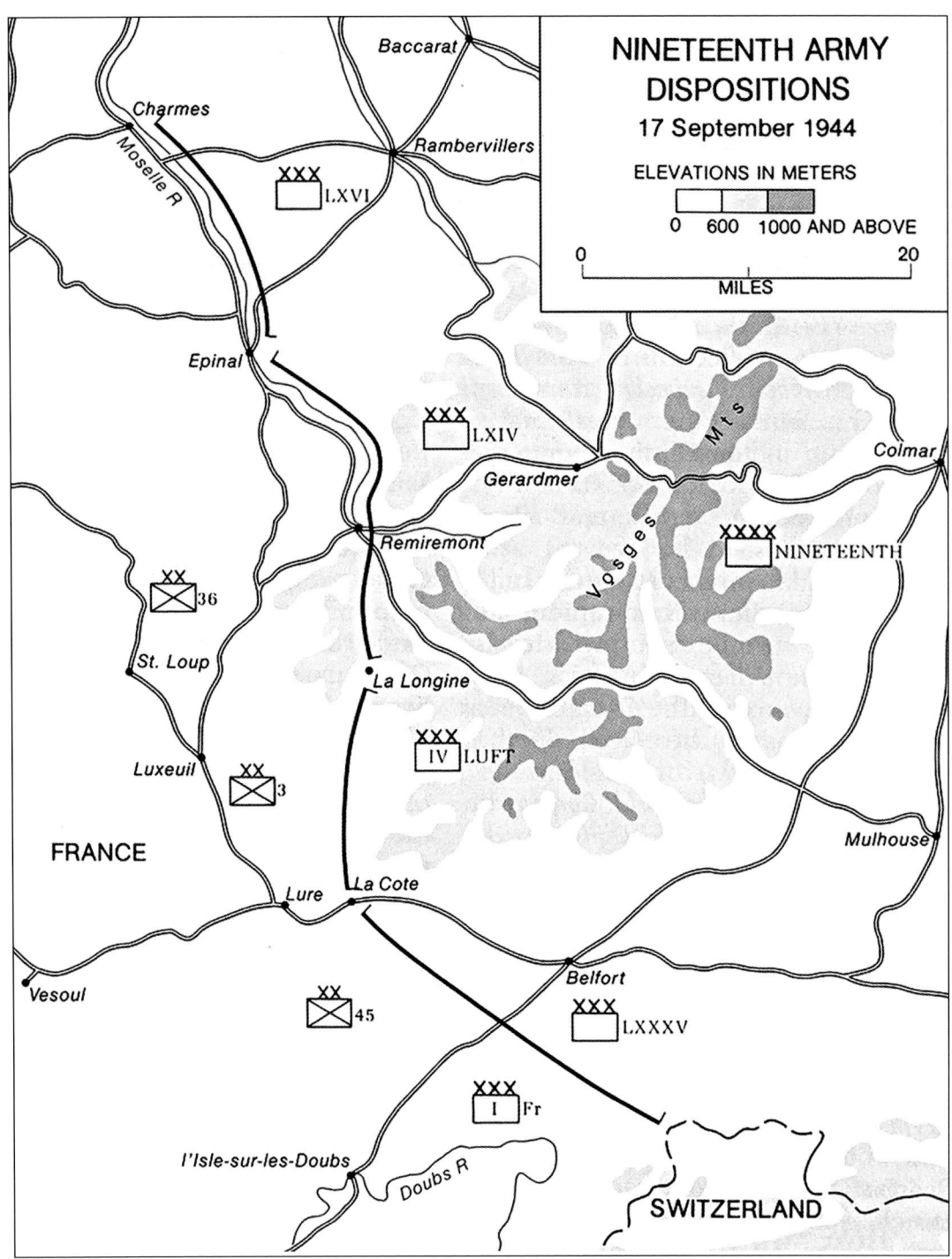

German dispositions in the Vosges and Alsace, September 17, a map from *Riviera to the Rhine*, the US Army Official History by Jeffrey J. Clarke and Robert Ross Smith.

Finally, at the southern end of Wiese's front, the LXXXV. Armeekorps was responsible for holding the approaches to Belfort and blocking the Belfort gap with, from north to south, the 159. and the 189. Infanterie-Divisions, both relatively fresh if understrength, and the desperately weak 338. Infanterie-Division. The 159. Infanterie-Division faced the southern wing of the IIème Corps d'Armée and the other two confronted the Ier Corps d'Armée. In static defensive positions to the rear, Festung-Brigade Belfort held the city of that name and the old forts that surrounded it. The brigade comprised two fortress artillery battalions and several fortress machine-gun companies but many of its guns were captured French and Russian pieces for which little ammunition was available. It had just received 30 of the potent 88mm anti-tank guns but some vital parts, such as the gun sights, still awaited delivery. On November 7, Ob. West informed Balck that the LXXXV. Armeekorps headquarters was to be transferred to Heeresgruppe B and on the 14th Generalkommando Dehner arrived to take its place. Until then this skeletal staff had controlled provisional units along the Swiss border and though it was promoted to the status of army corps on November 18, becoming LXIII. Armeekorps, it still lacked the normal corps support units.

General der Infanterie Friedrich Wiese was appointed commander of the 19. Armee in June 1944. This photo of him was taken in the spring of 1944 when he was already a holder of the Oak Leaves (awarded to him on January 24, 1944). He was awarded the Knight's Cross in February 1942 as commander of an infantry regiment on the Eastern Front. (Society for the study of the ETO)

Wiese's army had virtually no reserves from Colmar south to the Swiss border. He could only call on the NCO training centre at Colmar – 1,500 men in all, counting cadets, instructors and staff – and on the 30. SS-Waffen-Grenadier-Division, stationed near Mulhouse waiting for transportation east across the Rhine. This unit of conscripted Russian nationals had mutinied in September and though it had been reorganised with a more-substantial German cadre (one German to three Russians) it was still considered unreliable.

The German weakness in the Belfort sector reflected a major difference of opinion between Generals Balck and Wiese regarding the intentions of the French. While Wiese was convinced that they would soon attack in the Belfort gap itself, where the terrain was better, Balck thought that they would resume their advance across the Vosges, aiming for Colmar. Once they had reached the Alsatian plain, so he believed, the French would turn south to attack the Belfort gap from the rear. Any direct attack toward the gap, Balck believed, was only an effort to divert his attention away from a major threat across the Vosges. Accordingly, he insisted that Wiese keep two of his best divisions, the 198. and 269. Infanterie-Divisions, in the Vosges mountains. As a result, the flat and difficult to defend area south of Belfort (the focal point of the actual French attack) was left to the weak 338. Infanterie-Division which had only two regiments, both rated suitable for static defence only, and was short of artillery. All its infantry was deployed in its thin front line and it had no reserves.

THROUGH THE BELFORT GAP

In early November, Général de Lattre had both his corps in the line with two infantry divisions each, having withdrawn his two armoured divisions for rest and refitting. On the 1ère Armée's left, Général de Monsabert's IIème Corps d'Armée faced the mountains and narrow passes of the Vosges with, from north to south, the 3ème Division d'Infanterie Algérienne (DIA) and the 1ère Division de Marche d'Infanterie (DMI). On the right, Général Émile Béthouart's Ier Corps d'Armée was confronting the German defences of the Belfort gap. Guarding its left flank was a provisional force, Groupement Molle; in the centre, up to the Doubs river, was the 2ème Division d'Infanterie Marocaine (DIM); and on the right wing, from the Doubs to the Swiss border, was the 9ème Division d'Infanterie Coloniale (DIC).

Béthouart's corps was to launch the main effort on November 13, with the 2ème DIM first driving eastward to the Lizaine valley and then seizing Belfort with a surprise attack from the south. Failing that, the division was to sweep round Belfort on the north and south, attacking the metropolitan area and the surrounding forts from the rear. De Lattre had reinforced the 2ème DIM with two armoured combat commands of the 5ème Division Blindée, CC4 and CC5. On the corps' right wing, the 9ème DIC – with tank reinforcement provided by CC2 of the 1ère Division Blindée – was to press north-eastward to the general line of the Allaine river between Morvillars and Delle.

The IIème Corps d'Armée, on the left, was at first to maintain strong pressure along its front to keep the German attention focused on the Vosges. Depending on developments in the Ier Corps d'Armée sector, it was ultimately to drive across the mountain range and link up with the Ier Corps d'Armée in the vicinity of Mulhouse.

During the night of November 9/10, the Ier Corps d'Armée attack units began moving up to their start lines. However, continued rains had made the roads impassable for wheeled or even tracked vehicles and many temporary bridges had been washed out. On the 11th, Général Béthouart suggested postponing the attack until the weather improved and de Lattre finally approved some changes. Agreeing with Béthouart that the 9ème DIC might be better able to contend with the mud, rain, snow and increasingly cold weather than the 2ème DIM, they pushed the start of the latter's attack back

The French Ier Corps d'Armée started its offensive to breach the Belfort gap on November 14 with the 2ème Division d'Infanterie Marocaine attacking at midday. Two days later, advance units of the division, with elements of the 5ème Division Blindée in support, reached a point one kilometre short of Héricourt and the Lizaine river. These two Shermans of the 5ème Division Blindée were knocked out that day as they entered Issans, five kilometres south of Héricourt. (USNA)

The same spot in Issans today. The picture at the top of this page had been taken two days after the battle by which time the two disabled tanks had already been moved from the spot where they had been hit in order to clear the road.

The Battle of Alsace • 201

to the 14th. De Lattre also instructed Béthouart to move his armour forward on the 14th, earlier than planned, so as to be ready to exploit any success the two infantry divisions might achieve.

When November 13 dawned after hours of heavy snow, a complete lack of visibility forced the cancellation of the 9ème DIC's attack. Next morning, November 14, low clouds continued to cover much of the sector but some of it cleared north of the Doubs and de Lattre and Béthouart again quickly adjusted their plans. The 2ème DIM was directed to attack at midday after a two-hour artillery preparation, their attack to be followed by the left wing of the 9ème DIC at 1400 hours.

That very morning, Generalleutnant Friederich-August Schack, the newly appointed commander of the LXIII. Armeekorps, decided to have a personal look at the front. Having picked up Generalmajor Hans Oschmann, the commander of the 338. Infanterie-Division, he drove to an observation post near Bretigney, ten kilometres west of Montbéliard. Suddenly, the French artillery began a devastating barrage that immobilised their party for over two hours. As they started back eastward through woods turned into shambles by the gun barrage, they bumped into small groups of advancing French infantry. Oschmann was killed and the Generals' two aides captured, but Schack managed to escape, getting back to his command post at Belfort

By November 1944, all three French armoured divisions that had been equipped by the Americans were fighting with the 6th Army Group: the 2ème Division Blindée was operating on the left wing under the US XV Corps of the Seventh Army, and the 1ère and 5ème Divisions Blindées were on the right with the 1ère Armée. These Shermans of the 2ème Régiment de Cuirassiers, part of CC1 of the 1ère Division Blindée, were pictured in November 1944. (ECPAD)

before dark. Documents captured by the French soldiers revealed that Oschmann, far from expecting a major attack, had concluded that the French were digging in for the winter.

The left wing of the 2ème DIM gained little ground against the 189. Infanterie-Division but in the centre and on the right the French attack broke through the lines of the 338. Infanterie-Division and advanced over three kilometres. On the right, with its attack delayed until 1400 hours, the 9ème DIC found the units of the 338. Infanterie-Division south of the Doubs on the alert, yet pushed forward. In the evening, while army commander Wiese directed the LXIV. Armeekorps to disengage the 338. Infanterie-Division's third regiment from the Saint-Dié area and speed it back to the Belfort front, corps commander Schack decided to release his only reserve, three infantry battalions, in support of the 338. Infanterie-Division. The French continued their advance on the 15th and that evening, faced with the complete disorganisation of the 338. Infanterie-Division, Wiese had to approve a limited withdrawal to the Lizaine river.

Previously slowed by poor roads and extensive minefields, the French armour joined the battle on November 16. On the left, the 2ème DIM, now backed by elements of the 5ème Division Blindée, closed in on Héricourt and the Lizaine river. On the 17th, bridgeheads were established across the Lizaine between Luze, Héricourt and Montbéliard. On the right, supported by CC2 and CC3 of the 1ère Division Blindée, the 9ème DIC gathered momentum and progressed five kilometres on the 16th to reach Abbevillers the following day.

De Lattre and Béthouart now issued new orders. The 1ère Division Blindée was directed to assemble in the Abbevillers–Hérimoncourt area and strike east between the Rhône-Rhine Canal and the Swiss border. The 9ème DIC was to mop up behind the armour, secure the left flank and seize bridgeheads across the canal. Once bridges were in place, they planned to have the whole 5ème Division Blindée over the canal, bypass the urban area of Belfort on the east and exploit north-east toward Cernay and Colmar.

Meanwhile, the difference of opinion between Balck and Wiese as to the importance of the French operations around Belfort still had a paralysing effect on the German reaction. It was not until the evening of the 17th, and probably because of pressure from Ob. West, that Balck finally agreed that these operations were significant. He then approved the movement of the 198. Infanterie-Division and one regiment of the 269. Infanterie-Division to the Belfort gap. He also gave Wiese permission to pull the LXIII. Armeekorps back to a new line of defence from Héricourt south-east to the Swiss border, a measure that would greatly reduce the frontage to be held. The 338. Infanterie-Division began withdrawing after midnight with plans to reform along the Allaine river but dawn of the 18th found the troops still retreating east. The French gave no respite and, while the Germans succeeded to hold their new lines at Morvillars, the 1ère Division Blindée broke into the Allaine valley to the south and pushed north across the river.

On November 19, CC3 of the 1ère Division Blindée struck from the sector of Courtelevant and pushed eastward in three columns through Seppois and Waldighofen. Advancing along minor roads, a small detachment under Lieutenant Jean de Loisy made good progress and late in the afternoon these M5 light tanks of the 5ème Régiment de Chasseurs d'Afrique were pictured at Kappelen, less that ten kilometres from the Rhine river. (ECPAD)

A low sun rises over Kappelen on a beautiful winter morning. The restaurant on the left is still in business under the same 'two keys' name, although the German version of 1944, 'Gasthaus zu den zwei Schlüsseln', has since been turned into French: 'Café aux deux clefs'.

The French advance continued the next day, November 19, when CC3 started out from Courtelevant before dawn, moving eastward in three columns. Pushing through Seppois and over the Largue river, the armoured spearheads soon reached Waldighofen, only 20 kilometres from the Rhine river. In the afternoon an advance detachment heading on along small roads avoided the German defences and at about 1800 hours reached the Rhine near Rosenau, 100 kilometres south of Strasbourg. More forces followed and some shells were soon fired across the Rhine, the first French artillery fire to hit Germany since 1940.

De Lattre received another piece of good news in the evening when 6th Army Group made known that Devers had again been able to postpone the departure of the 1ère Division Blindée for the Atlantic coast, this time until mid-December.

On the German side, the situation in the evening of the 19th was such that General Wiese considered abandoning Belfort and pulling his army's southern flank all the way north to Mulhouse. However, von Rundstedt refused to give up Belfort and directed Balck not only to hold the city but to mount a counter-attack south of it to cut off the French penetration.

The 9ème DIC failed to secure crossings over the Rhône-Rhine Canal (Grenadier-Regiment 490 had just reached the front and deployed defensively on the canal), making it impossible for the 5ème Division Blindée to begin the planned drive toward Cernay, so de Lattre ordered the 1ère Division Blindée, further to the left, to push north from the point where it had reached the Rhine to the town of Chalampé where there were rail and road bridges across the river. He was still confident that the 5ème Division Blindée would cross the Rhône-Rhine Canal on the 20th and start north toward Colmar, parallel with the 1ère Division Blindée's advance along the Rhine.

Knowing from his own sources (he was not an 'Ultra' recipient) that the 198. Infanterie-Division had moved out of the Vosges, de Lattre expected it to shortly join the battle in the Belfort gap and so he gave the 9ème DIC the task of securing and enlarging the slender penetration to the Rhine.

The 198. Infanterie-Division had actually assembled a regimental combat team in the Dannemarie area and late on the 19th it launched a counter-attack southward toward Delle. By next morning, the lead units had reached the towns of Brebotte, Vellescot and Suarce – about halfway to Delle – when they ran into French armour and infantry deploying for an attack toward Dannemarie and inconclusive fighting took place throughout the afternoon. To the east, elements of the 30. SS-Waffen-Grenadier-Division had also attacked hoping to retake Seppois. They reached a point two kilometres north of it but then had to withdraw under French pressure.

Early on the 20th, the 2ème DIM penetrated into the city of Belfort and began the slow process of eliminating the last German defenders.

While CC2 and the 9ème DIC turned back the German counter-attack, the rest of the 1ère Division Blindée started its drive north. From 1330 hours, CC3

It was about 1830 hours on the 19th when Loisy's detachment reached the Rhine between Rosenau and Huningue. As so often with this kind of pictures, it is difficult to tell whether this shot of soldiers rushing to the river bank and dropping their unit flag into the water shows the genuine 'first reach' or a second or a third, or even a later re-enactment. (ECPAD)

The same length of river bank nearly 60 years later. A plaque (behind the photographer) now records the death of Sous-Lieutenant Jean Pierre Douzou, killed on this spot on November 30, 1944.

struck north-west toward Mulhouse from Bartenheim, five kilometres west of the Rhine at Rosenau. The armoured task force met little opposition and its leading elements soon pushed into the part of Mulhouse that lies south of the Rhône-Rhine Canal. Meanwhile, on the left, CC1 had driven to Altkirch, 15 kilometres to the south-west of Mulhouse, and by dark its lead units were inside the city. The following day, November 21, after a sharp encounter with elements of the 30. SS-Waffen-Grenadier-Division, CC1 cleared Altkirch and advanced farther north along the Rhône-Rhine Canal to Illfurth. That same day, CC3 at Mulhouse crossed the canal and cleared most of the city on the north bank.

The commitment of CC1 and CC3 at Altkirch and Mulhouse had left only a small force of the 1ère Division Blindée along the Rhine. Consisting of an armoured infantry company and a tank destroyer platoon, Détachement Colonnier nevertheless embarked on the task of driving north to Chalampé intending to seizing the Rhine bridges there. The force started out from Kembs on the 20th and arrived at the southern outskirts of Ottmarsheim, five kilometres south of Chalampé the following morning. However, the Germans counter-attacked on the 23rd and the small detachment had to withdraw. The French would not come any closer to Chalampé for another two and a half months.

On November 21, while the French were struggling to untangle CC2 and CC4 from the many traffic jams that blocked the roads all the way back to Montbéliard, the 198. Infanterie-Division moved and cut the vital N463 road near Courtelevant, in the rear of CC2. Elements of CC4 cleared the roadblock by noon but the Germans soon cut the road again and CC4 could only

The Battle of Alsace • 207

More troops soon followed and joined up with Lieutenant de Loisy on the Rhine bank. This M8 Gun Motor Carriage – a 75mm howitzer mounted on the chassis of an M5 light tank – might be the one that fired a few shells across the Rhine that day, historically the first French artillery fire to hit Germany since the Blitzkrieg days of 1940. (ECPAD)

The borders of France, Germany and Switzerland join here and the oil tanks seen across the Rhine are actually in the latter country. The street in Huningue leading to this spot is aptly named Rue des Trois Frontières, the street of the three frontiers.

The German 198. Infanterie-Division counter-attacked the French early on November 21 with one company of Panzerjäger-Abteilung 654 in support and cut the road near Courtelevant, eight kilometres east of Delle, in the rear of CC2 of the 1ère Division Blindée. This Jagdpanther of Panzerjäger-Abteilung 654 was lost during that operation. Though it cannot be seen in this picture, its tactical number was '122', showing it to belong to 2. Zug (platoon) of the 1. Kompanie. By noon, CC4 had cleared the enemy road-block but the Germans soon cut the road again and CC4 could only re-open it late in the afternoon. (ECPAD)

The French Army archives have no precise caption for the picture of Jagdpanther 122. However, thanks to a wartime report by Leutnant Enghoffer of Panzerjäger-Abteilung 654, the author was able to trace the unit's movements in Alsace and he finally found that No. 122 had been disabled at Lepuis-Neuf, three kilometres north of Courtelevant. Arriving from the direction of Suarce, it reached this crossroads from the right and was turning left when it was hit in the flank or rear by French fire coming from the southern entrance of the hamlet, the Courtelevant road.

re-open it late in the afternoon. These temporary interdictions of the supply lines of the 1ère Division Blindée greatly hampered the French effort to project more strength along the Rhine.

The 198. Infanterie-Division, with elements of Panzerjäger-Abteilung 654 in support, continued its southward counter-attack on the 22nd and its Grenadier-Regiment 308 took Réchésy and Pfetterhouse in the morning. The French halted their thrust from Pfetterhouse to Seppois, as they quickly moved to stop elements of the 30. SS-Waffen-Grenadier-Division heading

The Battle of Alsace • 209

Facing strong resistance, the 2ème Division d'Infanterie Marocaine slowly fought its way into the western and northern parts of Belfort on November 20. This picture was taken two days later when its leading elements were about to reach the bridges across the Savoureuse river in the centre of the town. German snipers are firing at these troops as they cautiously go forward. An M5 light tank from Combat Command 6 of the 5ème Division Blindée lends a hand. (USNA)

The building has been razed to the ground and the plot between the Quai Schneider and the Savoureuse river (off to the right) is now a parking lot.

for Seppois. Expecting that Panzerbrigade 106 and Sturmgeschütz-Brigade 280 would reach the sector during the day to assist, Wiese directed the 198. Infanterie-Division to move out on the 23rd without waiting for the armour. He also ordered the 30. SS-Waffen-Grenadier-Division on the left wing to resume its southward attack against Seppois.

However, the SS troops came across CC1 of the 1ère Division Blindée and made no progress on the 23rd. Meanwhile, on the right, Grenadier-Regiment 308 pressed on and succeeded to again cut the N463, this time

While the forward troops were fighting to take the bridges before the Germans could blow them (many bridges were in fact taken intact), Belfort west of the Savoureuse was being cleared from what Germans remained. (USNA)

The author was dicing with death when he took this comparison right in the middle of a junction on Avenue du Général Leclerc.

west of Seppois, and to control the roads in and out of Switzerland to the south. The lead units of the 198. Infanterie-Division were now dangerously overextended and could only hold these positions if the promised armoured elements arrived in the afternoon. But nothing came. Transportation problems had halted the movement of Sturmgeschütz-Brigade 280 and Balck had sent Panzerbrigade 106 elsewhere. Having learnt that a bridge across a canal in the middle of the Harth forest had been recaptured, he had directed the brigade to use that bridge, bypass Mulhouse on the east, make

The Battle of Alsace • 211

An M5 light tank of Combat Command 3 of the 1ère Division Blindée rolls into Mulhouse on November 21. The greater part of this French city lies south of the Doller river. By the evening, all of this had been conquered except for one small area in the east where the Germans had dug in around a barracks. (ECPAD)

Mulhouse is a large city and, with the road signs in the wartime picture being too general to give any clue, it was not easy to find where it was taken. It turned out to be on this corner on Rue Aristide Briand.

This M3 half-track was knocked out in Mulhouse on November 21 when the French assaulted one of the German strong points before falling back to wait for reinforcements. The picture was taken the following day. (USNA)

The author had another difficult search across the city before he finally found that the building still exists on Rue de Colmar.

a feint toward the area between Altkirch and Mulhouse, and then drive to Seppois. The armoured brigade made piecemeal advances during the afternoon of the 23rd but its leading elements soon became engaged in a lengthy duel with CC2 and were unable to advance southward.

The non-arrival of the expected armoured support sealed the fate of Grenadier-Regiment 308 for the French regained control of the N463 during the afternoon, thus isolating the regiment from the rest of the 198. Infanterie-Division north of the road. On November 24, the French swept the Réchésy–Pfetterhouse area and what was left of the German regiment, less than 300 men, crossed the border into Switzerland to be interned.

On November 22, impressed by the progress of the 1ère DMI in the Vosges, de Lattre had issued ambitious orders for a general exploitation calling for the IIème Corps d'Armée to push east across the Vosges, through the Bussang and Schlucht passes, and take Cernay. Once the Ier and IIème Corps d'Armée had linked up, they would then drive north to Colmar and

The fight for the barracks continued on November 22 and this picture was taken after tanks and infantry had assaulted what is described as the Gestapo barracks. (USNA)

The old barracks have been replaced by a new fire brigade building.

Strasbourg. However, when he learned on the 24th that the 1ère DMI would be pulled out within a few days to move to the Atlantic coast, de Lattre realised that his plans were too ambitious. He issued new instructions, ordering a double envelopment by the Ier and IIème Corps d'Armée with the pincers to close at Burnhaupt. The manoeuvre started at dawn on November 25 and the pincers closed at Burnhaupt on the afternoon of the 28th, after much bitter fighting. The operation was a clear success, bagging some 10,000 German prisoners.

The last German defenders evacuated Mulhouse on November 25, the same day that they evacuated Belfort, and the end of November saw the French consolidating their gains in and around Belfort, while the Germans were building up new defences along the line of the Doller river west of Mulhouse and holding tenaciously to the mountainous terrain north of Masevaux.

From positions in Rue Vauban, in front of the Sainte Jeanne d'Arc Church, Sherman tanks of the 2ème Régiment de Chasseurs d'Afrique fire from point-blank range at the Lefebvre barracks, one of the last points of resistance in Mulhouse, on November 23. The tanks will soon charge through the gates but the last German defenders were not to evacuate the barracks before the night of November 24/25. (USNA)

A corner of Mulhouse which has changed little.

The Battle of Alsace • 215

TAKING STRASBOURG

The objectives set by the US XV Corps for the November offensive were to capture Sarrebourg, force the Saverne gap, and prepare to exploit east of the Vosges. With cavalry forces covering along the Rhine-Marne Canal, the US 44th Division was to make the main effort initially and seize Sarrebourg from the west and north. The US 79th Division would then join in and the two divisions were to continue the offensive to the north-east and east. The French 2ème Division Blindée, placed under command of the American corps, would remain in corps reserve as exploitation force, ready to strike for the Saverne gap when the infantry divisions had begun breaking through the German defences.

The XV Corps attack would meet elements of three Volksgrenadier divisions: north of the Rhine-Marne Canal was part of the 361. Volksgrenadier-Division under LXXXIX. Armeekorps (1. Armee) while south of the waterway were the 553. and half of the 708. Volksgrenadier-Divisions under LXIV. Armeekorps (19. Armee). Knowing that neither German corps had any mobile reserves, the American corps commander, Major General Wade H. Haislip, expected that the enemy defence would be spotty and so he instructed his division commanders to have their lead units bypass isolated strong points and leave them to follow-up forces.

By the evening of November 12, wet snow blanketed the corps sector, streams were flooded and many roads and bridges were under water, and General Devers entertained thoughts of postponing the attack. However, gambling that the Germans might not expect an attack under such adverse conditions, he finally decided to go on.

The 44th Division jumped off on schedule early on November 13, attacking along the railway line to Sarrebourg behind a strong artillery preparation, with the 324th Infantry Regiment on the left and the 71st Infantry on the right. The men of the 553. Volksgrenadier-Division quickly recovered from the bombardment and responded with heavy and accurate artillery, mortar and machine-gun fire. The gains during the day were disappointing as were the operations on the following day.

Major General Robert L. Spragins, the 44th Division commander, then decided to commit his reserve, the 114th Infantry, on a northern swing, across the front of the other two regiments, sweeping through the German defences from the flank and rear. The manoeuvre proved successful and by the evening of the 15th had completely disrupted the 553. Volksgrenadier-Division. The 114th Infantry and the 106th Cavalry Group mopped up the left flank on the 16th, and the next day the 324th and 71st Infantry resumed their advance east, passing through the 114th which then reverted back into reserve. On the 19th, pushing along the axis of the N4, the 71st Infantry came within sight of the Marne Canal, ten kilometres short of the division's objective, Sarrebourg.

South of the 44th Division, the 314th Infantry of the 79th Division had

The attack by US XV Corps to force the Saverne gap began on November 13, the US 44th and 79th Divisions each jumping off with two regiments abreast. On the 16th, to ensure that the offensive maintained its momentum, Major General Wade Haislip, the corps commander, in addition committed elements of the French 2ème Division Blindée. The following day, the division's Groupement Tactique V (GTV) struck east from Montigny and seized Badonviller, the key to the whole German defence in the sector, and the right wing of the 708. Volksgrenadier-Division collapsed on the 18th. These elements of the 1er Régiment de Spahis were pictured in Brouville, 12 kilometres west of Badonviller, on November 17. (USNA)

One building has been razed to the ground and the pile of manure in front of the farmhouse has gone but otherwise the passage of 59 years has brought very little change to this part of Brouville.

The Battle of Alsace • 217

On November 19, General Haislip turned loose the 2ème Division Blindée, with the town of Saverne as its first objective, and Général Leclerc started off with two combat commands, GTD on the left and GTL on the right. Task Force Rouvillois, the northern column of GTD, struck east early on November 21, crossed the main north-south RN61 highway at Siewiller and pushed on as far as La Petite-Pierre, in the heart of the Low Vosges. Behind the French task force, the US 106th Cavalry Group secured the left flank, taking Baerendorf, Weyer and Drulingen. (ECPAD)

The two road signs faintly visible in the wartime picture, pointing to Eschwiller on one side and Drulingen on the other, enabled the author to trace the scene to Weyer, 12 kilometres west of La Petite-Pierre.

218 • OPERATION 'DRAGOON' AND BEYOND – THEN AND NOW

Another French Army photograph, probably taken on the same day, of men of the 2ème Division Blindée in Weyer. (ECPAD)

reached Halloville on November 14, while the 315th Infantry on the right had pushed toward Badonviller. The 708. Volksgrenadier-Division prepared a counter-attack to hit the Halloville penetration but a force of the 315th Infantry backed by tanks and tank destroyers struck first into the German assembly area east of Halloville. The surprised German reserves were dispersed and most of the 708. Volksgrenadier-Division's assault guns were lost in the failure. The Germans made two more attempts to restore the situation in the sector on the 15th, none with any success, and the 79th Division took Harbouey and continued its advance toward Sarrebourg.

During the night of November 15/16, the left wing of the 553. Volksgrenadier-Division fell back in good order to Blâmont and re-established a defensive line on the Vezouse river while the disorganised right wing of the 708. Voksgrenadier-Division occupied the line south of Cirey-sur-Vezouse.

To ensure that the offensive maintained its momentum, General Haislip

Though it was winter time when the author took this comparison, the lack of snow rather spoiled the seasonal atmosphere.

now committed the 2ème Division Blindée. One of its combat commands, Groupement Tactique R (GTR), began to push south-east from Halloville on November 16 and quickly disorganised the communication lines of the 708. Volksgrenadier-Division. Units of Groupement Tactique V (GTV) joined the attack the following day, seizing Badonviller. The right wing of the 708. Volksgrenadier-Division collapsed on the 18th enabling GTR and GTV to roll northward and capture bridges at Cirey. That same day, the 79th Division walked unopposed into Blâmont.

During the night of November 18/19, the left wing of the 553. Volksgrenadier-Division withdrew to establish a new defensive line from Richeval south and east through Tanconville and Lafrimbolle. The American and French attackers left the Germans no pause and by noon on the 19th, the 314th Infantry was nearing Richeval, the 315th had passed through Tanconville, and the spearheads of GTR were approaching Lafrimbolle in the mountains. At 1345 hours, Haislip turned the rest of the 2ème Division Blindée loose, with Saverne on the far side of the Vosges as immediate objective.

Général Leclerc (Philippe de Hauteclocque, nom de guerre Leclerc), the division commander, planned to lead off with two combat commands, GTD and GTL. After crossing the Rhine-Marne Canal, the two task forces of GTD were to bypass Sarrebourg to the west and north and head east across the Vosges well north of the Saverne gap. Once on the other side of the mountains, they were to descend on Saverne from the north and north-east. South of the canal, GTL, also with two columns, was to push east over small roads and cross the Vosges south of the Saverne gap. Having reached the Alsatian plains, the two task forces were to swing north to link up with GTD. The division's third combat command, GTR, would support GTL in the south and secure the division's extended right flank. The fourth combat command, GTV, would be in reserve, ready to reinforce either GTD or GTL. Upon relief by the 44th and 79th Divisions, the 2ème Division Blindée was to push on to Haguenau, about 20 kilometres north of Strasbourg. However, XV Corps warned Leclerc that he might have to withdraw back to Weyer, on the west side of the Vosges, should a threat develop on the corps' exposed northern flank.

Advancing in two separate columns, GTD crossed the Sarre river and pressed on meeting only weak German defences on the way. By late afternoon on the 21st its northern column, Task Force Rouvillois, had reached La Petite-Pierre, in the heart of the Vosges, and its southern arm, Task Force Quilichini, headed east until it was halted by well-defended anti-tank obstacles across the N4 in front of Phalsbourg.

South of Sarrebourg, GTL's northern column, Task Force Minjonnet, crossed the Sarre Rouge river on the 20th and drove eastward to Voyer, overrunning artillery positions of the 553. Volksgrenadier-Division and taking 200 prisoners. Farther south, Task Force Massu spent much of the morning of the 20th outflanking and breaking through the last defences of the 553. Volksgrenadier-Division along the Sarre Blanche river and finally captured Saint-Quirin in the afternoon. Commandant Jacques Massu then

Task Force Minjonnet, GTL's northern column, reached Saverne from the south-west on the morning of November 22 and quickly crossed the western part of the town to continue to its next objective ten kilometres to the north-west: the town of Phalsbourg. On their way, the French surprised and captured Generalmajor Hans Bruhn, the commander of the 553. Volksgrenadier-Division, and some of the LXXXIX. Armeekorps headquarters personnel. (ECPAD)

Luckily, the town of Saverne did not suffer too much damage during the war and these beautiful old houses near the town hall still remain.

sent his armour up the twisting mountain roads in the direction of the Valsberg pass.

Prisoners, mostly from artillery and service units, began to create a problem, especially for GTL's task forces south of Saverne, and XV Corps directed the 79th Division to attach two rifle companies to the 2ème Division Blindée to help handle the increasing number of surrendering Germans.

Knowing that his weak remaining forces were unable to interdict the Dabo road, Generalmajor Hans Bruhn, the commander of the 553. Volksgrenadier-Division, assembled 1,800 men, a few light artillery pieces and some vehicles in an area just north of Voyer late on the 20th. Aided by a heavy downpour, the group passed by several Allied outposts in the night and reached Arzviller before dawn on the 21st. Another force of some 300 men joined them in the morning, and with these two groups and miscellaneous other troops already in the area Bruhn began to organise the defences of the Saverne gap proper,

The Battle of Alsace • 221

As all this was going on, GTL's other column, Task Force Massu, which had broken out into the Alsatian plains the previous afternoon, had turned north in the morning and reached the eastern entrance of Saverne. Massu waited there for Task Force Minjonnet to clear the place and then entered the town from the east at 1400 hours. The Germans were taken completely by surprise and all the bridges in town were captured intact and over 800 prisoners taken. (ECPAD)

The Grande Rue in Saverne today, looking eastwards in the direction from where Massu arrived nearly six decades ago.

attempting to tie in his forces with the existing defences at Phalsbourg.

Starting out at dawn on the 21st, Task Force Massu reached the Valsberg pass by noon in spite of some resistance. Moving as fast as possible down the steep slopes of the eastern Vosges, the point units broke through to the Alsatian plains and Massu then turned north, heading for Saverne as planned. GTV, which followed behind, moved east, spreading out over the broad rolling terrain. Massu entered Saverne on the 22nd, capturing over 800 Germans, including Generalmajor Bruhn and some personnel of LXXXIX. Armeekorps headquarters.

General der Infanterie Gustav Hoehne, the new commander of the

LXXXIX. Armeekorps (dissatisfied with his performance, Balck had replaced General Werner von Gilsa), had just arrived that morning and, reviewing the situation, had immediately pulled most of his corps headquarters out of the town. Upon learning of Bruhn's capture, he took over what elements of the latter's 553. Volksgrenadier-Division he could find and, during the night of November 22/23, led them and his remaining corps staff northward along back roads through the mountains. They successfully crossed the D9 to La Petite-Pierre, stealthily slipping through between echelons of Task Force Quilichini.

While GTL (Task Forces Massu and Minjonnet recombined) and Task Force Rouvillois of GTD cleaned out Saverne and its environs on the 22d, GTV secured more Alsatian towns and villages south and south-east of the city, meeting little German resistance. Later in the afternoon, Minjonnet moved north-west up the N4 from Saverne and by dusk, having overrun many westward-facing German defences, was about two kilometres short of Phalsbourg.

The advance of the XV Corps in the Saverne gap and that of the Third Army's XII Corps just west of it might open a gap between the 1. and 19. Armee and Ob. West took measures to reinforce the threatened sector. Von Rundstedt had already directed Heeresgruppe H, in the Netherlands, to send the 256. Volksgrenadier-Division to the 1. Armee and on the 21st, he directed the same Heeresgruppe H to send another formation, the 245. Infanterie-Division. The former was weak, in the process of rebuilding, and the second was worn out.

On November 22 von Rundstedt gave Heeresgruppe G a provisional corps headquarters, known as Höheres Kommando Vogesen, to consolidate defensive preparations in the Strasbourg area. The new headquarters was to establish a line from the Moder river south to Wasselonne, 12 kilometres south-east of Saverne. As soon as it arrived at Haguenau, about November 24, the 256. Volksgrenadier-Division was to pass under its control but until then the forces at the disposal of Höheres Kommando Vogesen were insignificant: Feldkommandantur 987 (the regional Wehrmacht occupation command based at Haguenau); the armed forces command of Strasbourg; the headquarters (only) of the 49. Infanterie-Division; about 600 men from two infantry battalions; and miscellaneous small units that had begun to move westward across the Rhine.

Von Rundstedt knew that only a strong counter-attack could prevent an Allied breakthrough and he pressed the Oberkommando der Wehrmacht (OKW) to release the Panzer-Lehr-Division to him. Currently refitting in the rear, the Panzer-Lehr-Division had been earmarked for the Ardennes offensive and OKW was reluctant to authorise its commitment. Von Rundstedt finally succeeded in the afternoon of the 21st and the unit started south in the evening. However, OKW specified that it would have to return northward by November 28. Giving the Panzer-Lehr-Division to Heeresgruppe G, von Rundstedt directed Balck to commit it as a whole in a strong counter-attack

The 2ème Division Blindée continued to dash eastward on November 23 and Task Force Rouvillois entered Strasbourg at 1030 hours that morning. With the caption giving no clue whatsoever, the author faced a real challenge to find where this picture had been taken in the very large city of Strasbourg. (ECPAD)

He finally tracked down the location: the Allée David Goldschmidt in the Stockfeld part of the city. This is a southern quarter of Strasbourg, which means that the wartime picture was not taken during the initial advance into the city by Task Force Rouvillois, but later in the battle.

deep into the northern flank of the XV Corps' penetration. Balck drew up plans accordingly and in addition directed Wiese to organise a task force to link up with the Panzer-Lehr-Division from the south in the vicinity of Hazelbourg. Obviously, Balck had yet failed to appreciate that both the 553. and the 708. Volksgrenadier-Divisions were by then falling apart.

Having assembled near Sarre-Union, later than planned and with only

30 to 40 tanks and two of its four panzergrenadier battalions, the Panzer-Lehr-Division started southwards in the late afternoon of November 23. It attacked in two columns, the eastern one with 20 to 25 Panther tanks moving south through Eywiller and the western one with 10 to 12 PzKpfw IVs moving parallel down to Baerendorf. During the night, the western Kampfgruppe reached Rauwiller, taking 200 prisoners from the US 44th Division, and the eastern force pushed the US 106th Cavalry out of Weyer and south to Schalbach. The Americans were quick to react and on the morning of the 24th, CCB of the 4th Armored Division (from XII Corps, Third Army) moved eastwards across the Sarre into the XV Corps zone. The lead troops soon ran into the exposed flank of the western German force and house-to-house and tank-versus-tank fighting ensued in and near Baerendorf.

Just before dawn on the 25th, the western Kampfgruppe renewed its attack, hitting the CCB elements at Baerendorf and re-occupying part of Rauwiller. Confused fighting continued for several hours until the Germans finally fell back to the north and north-east. Meanwhile, the eastern Kampfgruppe had overrun part of the 2nd Battalion, 114th Infantry, of the 44th Division near Schalbach. However, strong American artillery fire turned back their efforts to advance further south. For all practical purposes, by the afternoon of the 25th the Panzer-Lehr-Division's offensive had been brought to a halt. Von Rundstedt called off the operation in the evening and the division withdrew northwards to temporary defensive lines between the Sarre river and Eywiller. With it, any danger to the XV Corps flank disappeared.

Strasbourg was a VI Corps objective but while that corps was still fighting its way through the Vosges, the city had come within easy reach of XV Corps and on the 21st, Patch ordered Haislip to 'attack Strasbourg, employing armoured elements to assist the VI Corps in the capture of the city.' After that Haislip was to push north along the Rhine to the Soufflenheim-Rastatt area, taking advantage of any opportunity to force a crossing. The VI Corps was to prepare to cross the Rhine in its sector or, more likely, to exploit through a XV Corps bridgehead. Consequently, on the morning of the 22nd, Haislip ordered the 2ème Division Blindée to strike for Strasbourg and secure the city if it reached the area before the VI Corps.

The official US Army historians, Clarke and Smith, described the capture of Strasbourg thus: 'Starting out about 0715 on November 23, GTL rolled rapidly eastward across the Alsatian plains with Task Force Rouvillois on the north and Task Force Massu to the south. Overrunning German outposts and minor garrisons in the small Alsatian farming towns, TF Rouvillois achieved complete surprise and entered Strasbourg at 1030 that morning. TF Massu, which was to have driven into the city from the north-west, encountered stronger German opposition, but ultimately followed shortly thereafter. Later, about 1300 that afternoon, GTV also began pouring into Strasbourg from the west, bringing with it a battalion of the 313th Infantry, 79th Division.

'Meanwhile, amid almost incredible scenes of German surprise and

With large official buildings in the background, this picture of a lorry burning after a hit from a German shell promised to be easier to find. It was probably taken the following day, November 24, when the Germans had recovered from their surprise and started to retaliate from across the Rhine. (USNA)

Strasbourg, Place de la République, today.

consternation, Rouvillois' armour wheeled through the streets of Strasbourg to the Rhine, seizing intact bridges over the canal-like watercourses in the eastern section of the city. Ahead lay the highway and railway bridges over the Rhine to the German town of Kehl scarcely 650 metres short of the river. However, the French armour ran into strongly manned German defences in apartment houses and thick-walled bunkers, buttressed by anti-

The sudden appearance of French armour in Strasbourg had caught the Germans completely off guard and hundreds of them were taken prisoner in the city. (ECPAD)

tank barriers and anti-tank weapons. Soon German artillery and mortars emplaced east of the Rhine began laying down accurate fire that forced Rouvillois' troops and vehicles to pull back and seek cover. The local German commanders had apparently ignored any instructions to outpost the Alsatian plains and instead had concentrated on defending certain sections of the city, including the vital Kehl bridges.

'Throughout November 23 and 24 TF Rouvillois made several attempts

Generalmajor Franz Vaterrodt (left), commanding general of the Wehrmacht forces in the Strasbourg area, sheltered in Fort Ney until November 25 when he finally surrendered with the 800 men that were with him. He is seen here later that day, with Major Roland H. McIntire (centre) of the US Seventh Army Headquarters, after he had been taken to Strasbourg. (USNA)

The Battle of Alsace • **227**

Following the fall of Strasbourg, the XV Corps bagged a total of 12,000 prisoners, including three generals. On November 24 or 25 these prisoners were put to work to dismantle the barricades and defence positions built in the city. (ECPAD)

Place Kléber, which the Germans had renamed Karl-Roos-Platz in 1940, as it looks today.

to reduce the German bridgehead, but the result was a stalemate. Lacking strength for an all-out assault in the urban area, the infantry-poor French armoured units had to be content with isolating the German enclave from the rest of the city. The Germans, in turn, made no move to reinforce or enlarge the bridgehead and, pending orders to destroy the bridges, held on mainly to aid the escape of German troops and civilians able to infiltrate through the French vehicles to safety. In the meantime, TF Massu and GTV mopped up isolated pockets of resistance, took hundreds of German troops prisoner and began rounding up German civilians for internment.'

As the 2ème Division Blindée was occupying Strasbourg's city centre without too much difficulty on the 23rd, other units of the division rushed on eastwards to the Rhine. However, a few hundred metres short of the road and rail bridges over the river they ran into strong German defences backed by anti-tank weapons. These two Shermans of the 12ème Régiment de Cuirassiers, Cherbourg and Meknes, were stopped dead in their tracks. (ECPAD)

By-passed by a new road leading to the new Rhine bridge – the Pont d'Europe – the Route du Rhin is now a quiet back street. Note how six of the trees lining the street have survived all these 60 years. In the background the Sainte Jeanne d'Arc Church also remains unchanged and the large building at left is still a school.

A Sherman tank today stands nearby as a memorial to Sergent-Chef Albert Zimmer, the commander of the Cherbourg, who was killed here when his tank was hit.

The liberation of Alsace, a French province that had been annexed by the Third Reich in 1940, was of great significance to the French and particularly to Général Leclerc, the commander of the 2ème Division Blindée. In March 1941, when he had just forced the Italian garrison of the Kufra oasis in Libya to surrender, then Colonel Leclerc had promised not to cease fighting before the tricolour flag fly again over Strasbourg and Metz. This small parade held on Place Kléber on November 26, 1944 was to celebrate the fulfilment of that promise. (ECPAD)

A perfect comparison on Place Kléber.

On annexation, Alsace-Lorraine became the German Gau of Elsass-Lothringen and Germanic names were quickly given to all the streets and squares in these provinces. In Strasbourg, Place Kléber became Karl-Roos-Platz (Karl Roos had been executed by the French in February 1940 as a German spy), Place Broglie was turned into Adolf-Hitler-Platz, and the Rue du 22 Novembre (the day when the French troops reached Strasbourg in 1918) was renamed Strasse des 19. Juni, after the day the Germans had entered the city in 1940. When Alsace was liberated, the removal of the Nazi signs became an urgent necessity. (ECPAD)

The November offensive of the 6th Army Group had crushed the 19. Armee in a giant pincer: while in the south the 1ère Armée had gained control of the Belfort gap and reached the Rhine, in the north the Seventh Army had crossed the Vosges and taken Strasbourg. In doing so, the Allied armies had nearly destroyed six of 19. Armee's eight infantry divisions: the 553. and 708. Volksgrenadier-Divisions on the approaches to Saverne; the 716. Infanterie- and 16. Volksgrenadier-Divisions in the Vosges; and the 338. and 198. Infanterie-Divisions in the Belfort gap. To defend Alsace, General Wiese could count only on two divisions which remained in fair condition, the 269. and the 159. Infanterie-Divisions, that were holding the Vosges mountains west of Colmar, plus two more that were coming from the Netherlands and a collection of personnel and miscellaneous units of no value. Nevertheless, on November 24 and 27 Hitler approved directives which committed the 19. Armee to the defence of a vast bridgehead west of the Rhine, a bridgehead that soon became known in the Allied camp as the Colmar Pocket.

NO RHINE CROSSING

Elated by their successful advance to Strasbourg and the Rhine and convinced that the 19. Armee would soon withdraw across the river, 6th Army Group and Seventh Army planners were speeding preparations for a Rhine crossing in the Rastatt area. Devers and Patch had previously envisaged a crossing sometime between December 10 and 20, but their thoughts now turned to the first week of December. A northward exploitation by VI Corps through a XV Corps bridgehead would begin no later than the second week of the month. Specialised river-crossing units had been alerted to move to forward assembly areas and by the afternoon of the 24th, amphibious DUKW companies were rolling toward the Rhine.

That day, November 24, Eisenhower and Bradley began a tour of the Allied southern front. They first visited Patton at Nancy and found Third Army nearly halted. The weather was awful, the ground had turned into a sea of mud, and traffic was breaking up the roads. Patton urged them that either a portion of his front be assigned to the 6th Army Group or the XV Corps be returned to Third Army control, preferably the latter. Bradley said he favoured narrowing the Third Army front but Eisenhower was noncommittal though he seemed to have also made up his mind. Eisenhower and Bradley next travelled to Lunéville where they picked up Devers and Patch before proceeding with them to Haislip's XV Corps headquarters at Sarrebourg and then to Brooks' VI Corps command post at Saint-Dié.

As described by Clarke and Smith in Riviera to the Rhine: 'Within both headquarters Eisenhower and Bradley found the corps staffs busily planning to push their forces farther east, seize bridgeheads over the Rhine and cross into Germany itself. Eisenhower, however, quickly ended these preparations. Concerned about Patton's flagging offensive, he wanted the Seventh Army's axis of attack reoriented from the east to the north, through the Low Vosges and against the German 1. Armee's southern flank. At Haislip's command post, he even issued verbal orders directing the XV Corps to halt all preparations for a Rhine crossing, change direction immediately and advance generally northward astride the Vosges mountains in close support of the Third Army. Supporting Patton's advance into the Saar basin was to have first priority.

'Somewhat stunned by the new orders, Devers was determined to challenge them. Returning to the 6th Army Group headquarters at the Héritage Hôtel in Vittel that evening, the three principal American ground commanders had a late formal dinner and then retired to Devers' private office to talk over the entire matter. The ensuing discussion lasted until the early hours of the following day and saw a heated argument between Eisenhower, Bradley and Devers. Eisenhower continued to insist that Devers halt all preparations for a Rhine crossing and turn the Seventh Army north to assist Patton's forces as quickly as possible. Although current SHAEF directives had provided for the opportunistic seizure of bridgeheads across the Rhine during the November

On November 24, after a heated argument between Eisenhower, Bradley and Devers at the 6th Army Group headquarters in Vittel, the Supreme Commander ruled firmly against a 6th Army Group crossing, even if current SHAEF directives had previously provided Devers for the opportunistic seizure of bridgeheads across the Rhine during the November offensive. Devers and his 6th Army Group staff had no other option than to swallow their disappointment and they turned their attacks northwards. This picture was taken at the command post of the French Ier Corps d'Armée at Beaucourt on November 25 when Eisenhower and Devers toured the French front with General Bradley. (L-R): Bradley; Général de Lattre, 1ère Armée; Général Emile Béthouart, Ier Corps d'Armée; Devers and Eisenhower. (ECPAD)

offensive by all participants, the Supreme Commander now ruled firmly against a Seventh Army crossing. Furthermore, he proposed transferring two divisions from the 6th Army Group to Bradley's 12th Army Group and extending the boundary of Haislip's XV Corps to the north-west. Devers objected bitterly to each of these measures, arguing that the Seventh Army was the force that ought to be strengthened and not the Third. If assisting Patton was the primary objective then, he contended, a Seventh Army Rhine crossing at Rastatt followed by a drive north to envelop the Saar basin was the best solution. On this point, however, Bradley strongly disagreed: attempting to force the Rhine against the prepared defensive positions of the West Wall was foolhardy and would only lead to failure. Exasperated, Devers countered that the Germans currently had few if any troops in front of the Seventh Army and that Patch's reconnaissance patrols across the Rhine had found the defences there completely unmanned. Eisenhower was unmoved. He instructed Devers to use whatever strength was necessary to clean up the area between the Vosges and the Rhine but to turn the Seventh Army north as quickly as possible, attacking west and east of the Low Vosges. There would be no Rhine crossing.'

Eisenhower reportedly came out of the Vittel conference 'mad as hell' over Devers' open criticism of his strategy. The following day he and Bradley concluded their visit in touring the French front before returning north via Vittel on the morning of the 26th. Devers, who openly wondered if he was 'a member of the same team', persisted in his opinion that Eisenhower's decision was a major error and that he ought to have instead reinforced the successful Seventh Army breakthrough to the Rhine. Also, while he agreed that the Third and Seventh Armies working together could easily breach the defences of the Saar, Devers judged that Third Army logically belonged in his own 6th Army Group.

The question remains what might have come out of a crossing of the Rhine in the south in late November or early December 1944. As Brigadier General Garrison H. Davidson, who in 1944 was the Seventh Army Chief Engineer, wrote 30 years after the event: 'I have often wondered what might have happened had [Eisenhower] had the audacity to take a calculated risk as General Patton would have instead of playing it safe. Perhaps success would have eliminated any possibility of the Battle of the Bulge; 40,000 casualties there could have been avoided and the war shortened by a number of months at the saving of other thousands of lives.' The Seventh Army, Davidson concluded, had 'provided [Eisenhower] with an opportunity to depart from his broad front strategy . . . and make a lightning thrust across the Rhine in the Strasbourg-Rastatt area.'

By the end of November 1944, the situation for the German forces in Alsace was quickly deteriorating. In the north, the US XV Corps had broken through the Saverne gap and reached Strasbourg, opening a gap between the 1. Armee and the 19. Armee, while in the south, French forces had reached the Rhine and the last defences in and around Belfort were about to collapse.

Judging that the Allied armies would probably attempt to encircle and destroy the 19. Armee by means of concurrent drives south from Strasbourg and north from Mulhouse, General Balck and General Wiese agreed that their southern flank had to be pulled back to the east and north immediately. General Balck gave this evaluation to the Ob. West, Generalfeldmarschall Gerd von Rundstedt, on the morning of November 24. That afternoon clearer information on the situation in the Saverne area arrived at the Ob. West HQ located in Coblenz as well as news of the failure of a counter-attack by the Panzer-Lehr-Division. As a result, von Rundstedt appealed to the Oberkommando der Wehrmacht (OKW – Armed Forces High Command) that without immediate reinforcements – at least two panzer divisions and one infantry division and both fully up to strength – it would be impossible to hold the situation in northern Alsace and close the gap between 1. Armee and 19. Armee. However, all available reserves were currently being husbanded for the scheduled Ardennes counter-offensive and OKW had no spare units available. Without reinforcements, and to avoid destruction, von Rundstedt and Balck concluded that the 19. Armee had no choice but to abandon the whole of Alsace and withdraw quickly across the Rhine.

The centre and right wing of the IIème Corps d'Armée were still fighting over some of the highest and most rugged hill masses of the Vosges. This picture of elements of the 3ème Régiment de Spahis Algériens, the reconnaissance unit of the 3ème Division d'Infanterie Algérienne, was taken some time after the capture of the Bonhomme Pass in mid-December. (ECPAD)

The author traced the spot where this picture had been taken at the Calvaire Pass at an altitude of 1144 metres, right on top of the summit of the Vosges, some five kilometres south of the Bonhomme Pass. Due west of Colmar, this pass brought one of the major roads across the High Vosges.

As far as Hitler was concerned this was totally out of the question. Not only could he not face the idea of giving up the re-annexed Alsace to the French; he was now being asked to consider cancelling his planned master stroke in the Ardennes in favour of a major counter-attack in Alsace and Lorraine. No, the 19. Armee was to continue the fight and those parts of Alsace still under German control were to be held at all costs.

Nevertheless, the situation on the northern and southern flanks of 19. Armee continued to deteriorate and by the afternoon of the 26th von

The Battle of Alsace • 235

The weak logistical machine of the 1ère Armée proved unable to sustain it in battle for any length of time and the rugged terrain made support even more difficult. One of the best methods of transporting supplies were pack mules like these belonging to the 1ère DMI as the beasts could negotiate the mountainous roads without undue trouble. (ECPAD)

Thanks to a road-sign reading 'Triembach' that appears in another shot from the same series, the author was able to determine where this picture was taken. It turned out to be in the hamlet of Hohwarth, on the D2 between Villé and Kogenheim, about ten kilometres north-west of Sélestat.

Rundstedt finally persuaded OKW to approve a new defensive line, one that was more or less the same as had been originally proposed by Balck. That night Hitler finally gave his assent and von Rundstedt issued the necessary orders in the early hours of the 27th.

The Hitler-approved directive of November 27 was committing the 19. Armee to the defence of a vast bridgehead west of the Rhine, a bridgehead that soon became known in the Allied camp as the Colmar Pocket. Initially, the salient had a base along the Rhine for 65 kilometres between Erstein

That ruling required a major regrouping of the Seventh Army and it was not before November 27 that the VI Corps finally moved off southwards with plans to clear the area from the Vosges mountains to the Rhine. Here, elements of the 2ème Division Blindée move southwards through the town of Entzheim, ten kilometres south-west of Strasbourg, on the 27th. (ECPAD)

The vehicles may have moved on but otherwise time has stood still at Entzheim.

and Mulhouse, and its centre extended more than 40 kilometres westward from the river into the Vosges mountains. OKW and Ob. West estimated that with some replacements and at least some anti-tank artillery and assault guns, the 19. Armee could hold the salient for about three weeks, a time span dictated by the date set for the launching of the Ardennes offensive. To this end, during the first days of December, Wiese strove to bolster the depleted combat units of his eight infantry divisions with a variety of military personnel scraped together from all branches and services.

Civilians cheer as tanks of the 2ème Division Blindée drive past their house in Entzheim. (ECPAD)

The Route de Strasbourg at Entzheim has remained remarkably unchanged.

On December 10, Hitler's determination to hold the salient was reaffirmed when he appointed Reichsführer-SS Heinrich Himmler to take command of Heeresgruppe Oberrhein, a new headquarters that had been set up to control the 19. Armee in Alsace and the motley collection of formations assembled over on the eastern bank of the Rhine. Heeresgruppe Oberrhein was treated as a separate theatre command and Himmler reported not to von Rundstedt's Ob. West but directly to OKW and to Hitler himself. However

While the 2ème Division Blindée and elements of the US 14th Armored Division started to push south, the US 103rd Division came down the Vosges from the west. This M7 Gun Motor Carriage – a 105mm howitzer mounted on the chassis of an M3 medium tank – of the artillery regiment of the 2ème Division Blindée was pictured as it entered the town of Obernai, 30 kilometres south-west of Strasbourg. (ECPAD)

Rue de Molsheim in Obernai today.

questionable his military abilities, Himmler was able to accelerate the infusion of replacements into both the Colmar area and the east bank defences by having the immediate German interior scoured more thoroughly for supplies, equipment and manpower. In addition, the direct presence of the chief of the police undoubtedly ensured that no unauthorised withdrawals occurred and local commanders were 'inspired' to defend each village or water crossing with determination. On December 15, Himmler

Sherman tanks from Combat Command A of the 14th Armored Division pass through Obernai on their way to Barr, ten kilometres further south. The lead units of this green division entered that town on the 28th, only to find themselves trapped in its narrow streets, losing 18 tanks in the process. (ECPAD)

Some patches of snow remaining on the roofs did their best to give our comparisons the desired winter atmosphere. This street leading to the town hall in the centre of the Obernai is now the Rue du Général Giraud.

On December 16 the 36th Division (with the 30th Infantry Regiment of the 3rd Division attached) took Kaysersberg, ten kilometres north-west of Colmar. The Germans counter-attacked on the 17th and house-to-house fighting raged in the village throughout the morning. To try to break the German effort, the IIème Corps d'Armée then sent one battle group of the 5ème Division Blindée to clear Kientzheim, the village east of Kaysersberg, from where the Germans hat set out. Capitaine Davout d'Auerstadt led his squadron into Kientzheim that afternoon where he waited for American infantry to join them to help clear the village. This picture of Fornoue, a Sherman M4A4 of the 1er Régiment de Chasseurs d'Afrique was taken on Place Schwendi in the centre of the village. (USNA)

Peace and quiet has now returned to Kientzheim.

replaced Wiese with General der Infanterie Siegfried Rasp as commander of the 19. Armee. One week later, on the 22nd, Generaloberst Blaskowitz replaced General Balck to command Heeresgruppe G.

Following the decision by General Eisenhower on November 24 to turn the main thrust of the US 6th Army Group northwards on the west bank of the Rhine – much to the disappointment of Devers and his staff – by December 5

The Battle of Alsace • 241

Eylau, an M10 tank destroyer of the 11ème Régiment de Chasseurs d'Afrique, was knocked out at the western entrance of Kientzheim. (ECPAD)

Nicely restored after having been destroyed on December 18 in the battle for Kientzheim, Renard, a Sherman of the 1er Régiment de Chasseurs d'Afrique, now stands almost exactly on the spot where Eylau was disabled.

they had switched the US Seventh Army north as ordered by SHAEF. When Devers and de Lattre were surprised by the efforts of the German 19. Armee to continue to hold in the Colmar pocket instead of simply pulling back across the Rhine, Devers wanted the 1ère Armée to renew its offensive against the pocket as soon as possible and finish the job of clearing southern Alsace. To achieve this, he decided to transfer operational control of the US 36th Infantry Division and the French 2ème Division Blindée from the Seventh Army to the 1ère Armée, effective December 5.

To clear the German enclave, de Lattre planned a two-pronged offensive with the French Ier Corps d'Armée attacking north through Cernay on December 13 and the French IIème Corps d'Armée with the 36th Infantry Division and the 2ème Division Blindée attached pushing south from the Sélestat area on the 15th. However, it was questionable whether the 1ère Armée was strong enough to carry out such an endeavour. The November battle had exhausted French manpower and materiel resources, a situation from which they had difficulty in recovering because of their weak logistical and personnel support systems. Efforts to turn FFI elements into regular units continued to have serious drawbacks and the recruiting and training of new personnel, especially officers and technicians, could not be accomplished overnight.

Also the strength of the 1ère Armée was still undermined by the demands of Operation 'Independence', the attempt to open the Gironde estuary which was the approach to Bordeaux, the major port in south-western France. Initially, it was planned to have the French 1ère Division Blindée departing for the Gironde operation on November 11 and the 1ère Division de Marche d'Infanterie (DMI) following on the 27th but, after a series of postponements, the 1ère DMI only started to move out on December 9. The 1ère Division Blindée was due to follow when, two days after the German attack in the Ardennes, SHAEF ordered another postponement. By then the main body of the 1ère DMI had reached western France and, though the division was quickly turned around, it arrived too late to play a part in the renewed offensive against Colmar.

By then the 36th Division and the 2ème Division Blindée – which had been assigned to reinforce the 1ère Armée – had both turned southwards. The 36th Division started to clean out the Kaysersberg valley but after ten days of heavy fighting it was so exhausted that its commander, Major General John E. Dahlquist, requested its immediate relief. With Devers' approval, the Seventh Army replaced it with the US 3rd Infantry Division on December 15.

In the meantime, with the armour of the 2ème Division Blindée having difficulty in moving in the water-soaked plains, its commander, Général Leclerc (Philippe de Hauteclocque), protested that his mission of clearing the area between the Rhine and Ill rivers was more appropriate for an infantry division. When Leclerc went to Paris to plead his case with Général de Gaulle, Devers considered either disbanding the unit or getting SHAEF

For several days, the Germans mounted repeated counter-attacks and the villages of Mittelwihr and Bennwihr, four kilometres east of Kientsheim, were taken, lost and retaken several times and it was not until December 25 that Bennwihr was finally secured by the 15th Infantry. Two days later Signal Corps photographer T/5 B. J. McCroby took this picture of a group of dead Germans lying at the side of the road. Observing how they were assembled when they fell, with no weapon visible and several of them without helmets, it seems likely that they were prisoners shot after having surrendered. They had belonged to the Begleit-Bataillon Reichsführer-SS (note the SS collar patch), one of the motley formations rushed to Alsace to bolster the 1. Armee. (USNA)

It was the details appearing on the road sign that led us to the correct location at the southern entrance of Beblenheim, just north of Mittelwihr.

to move it somewhere off his patch. In the end he finally told Leclerc that the 2ème Division Blindée had no choice but to accomplish the mission.

On December 15, shortly after the arrival of the 3rd Division, de Lattre renewed his offensive against the pocket, using the Ier Corps d'Armée to attack towards Cernay and the IIème Corps d'Armée striking through the Kaysersberg-Sélestat area. The cold, wet and overcast weather slowed down operations and made it impossible for vehicles to move off the roads, which

244 • OPERATION 'DRAGOON' AND BEYOND – THEN AND NOW

nullified de Lattre's numerical superiority in armour. That first day, neither corps was able to make more than a few dents in the now strengthened German defences.

News of the German offensive in the north spread rapidly through the 6th Army Group during the evening of December 16. At first, many commanders reasoned that the German initiative in the Ardennes would weaken their forces in the south, thereby offering the Seventh Army a unique opportunity to break through the Westwall. However, such optimistic thinking did not last long and the strength of the German offensive soon became clear. Late on the 18th, SHAEF ordered the US Third Army to despatch the 80th Infantry and 4th Armored Divisions northward for the Ardennes. At the same time, General Bradley, the 12th Army Group commander, instructed General Patton, the Third Army commander, to halt all preparations for his own offensive then scheduled for the following day and to prepare to send more of his divisions northward.

The next day, December 19, General Eisenhower held a major command conference at Verdun attended by Devers, Bradley and Patton at which he called for counter-attacks against the northern and southern shoulders of the German penetration in the Ardennes. Third Army was put in charge of the southern counter-strike (which would change its direction of advance from east to north), while Devers' 6th Army Group was to halt all offensive operations and take over responsibility for most of the sector vacated by the Third Army. Priority in supplies, equipment and manpower would go to the forces fighting in the Ardennes.

Consequently, Devers ordered the offensives against the Westwall and the Colmar pocket to end immediately. The Seventh Army was to occupy the extended front, spreading out to the west and north-west, and adopting a defensive posture, and the new boundary between the 12th and 6th Army Groups was to be moved over 40 kilometres west of the old November 26 line. As for the 1ère Armée, although it was to break off the action against Colmar, Devers directed de Lattre to be prepared to resume the offensive no later than January 5 by which time he expected the emergency in the north to be over.

As recounted by the official US Army historians Jeffrey J. Clarke and Robert Ross Smith in Riviera to the Rhine, 'privately General Devers was hardly pleased with the new orders. Recalling Eisenhower's decision on November 24 halting the Seventh Army's Rhine crossing in the Rastatt area, he felt that his command was once again being called on to bail out the northern army groups "just as we are about to crack the Siegfried Line by infiltration . . . which would permit us to turn both east and west, threatening Karlsruhe to the east and loosening up the entire Siegfried Line in front of the Third Army to the west".' Although recognising the necessity of turning the Third Army north against the German Ardennes offensive, Devers believed it a 'tragedy' that the Allied high command had 'not seen fit to reinforce success on this flank.'

On January 7, the LXIV. Armeekorps launched Operation 'Sonnenwende' to re-take a triangular area between the Ill and Rhine rivers near Erstein south of Strasbourg. No genuine photographs appear to have been taken during this operation although the author has identified this sequence lifted from film footage shot for the German Wochenchau newsreel that was shown to cinema audiences in late January 1945. In this still we see grenadiers of the 198. Infanterie-Division on January 7 as they move into Obenheim, one of the villages recaptured during this German counter-attack. (Die Deutsche Wochenschau)

OPERATION 'SONNENWENDE'

By the end of December, when the momentum of Heeresgruppe B's attack in the Ardennes had begun to peter out, the German command realised that the Allies had greatly weakened their southern army group to counter the attack

Rue Voegele in Obenheim, eight kilometres south-east of Erstein, looking northwards.

in the Ardennes. As a result, the Germans believed that a new offensive in the south could exploit this weakness or, at least, bring some relief to their hard-pressed forces in the north. Accordingly, plans were made and it was finally agreed that the 1. Armee was to launch two attacks on New Year's Eve, one down the Sarre valley and the other through the Vosges. As for Heeresgruppe Oberrhein, it was to launch supporting attacks north and south of Strasbourg.

Heeresgruppe Oberrhein began on January 5 by attacking across the Rhine at Gambsheim north of Strasbourg. Two days later, the 19. Armee initiated another assault south of the city near Rhinau, on the northern edge of the Colmar pocket. The initial objectives of this operation, which was code-named 'Sonnenwende' (Winter Solstice), were limited and consisted of a triangular zone between the Ill and Rhine rivers from Sélestat to Erstein. Then, in a second phase, the advance was to reach Molsheim, another 15 kilometres northward, until eventually Strasbourg was invested.

Charged with the initial assault, the LXIV. Armeekorps commander, General der Infanterie Hellmuth Thumm, had concentrated his attack on

With no indication as to the location, and the date questionable, the identification of clips from news film is not easy. The author comments that 'when I saw this short sequence showing German troops proudly posing with a captured French car I reasoned that it might have been taken in an area just recaptured from French forces. This narrowed down the search as there were not that many and I circled the area south of Strasbourg where a dozen villages had been recaptured during the "Sonnenwende" operation'. (Die Deutsche Wochenschau)

The Battle of Alsace • **247**

'I started to work from north to south, visiting each village in turn, and was lucky to find the location in the third village I looked at: Obenheim. The decisive clue was this house on the corner of the street in the shot showing a Bergepanther towing a Jagdpanther of schwere Panzerjäger-Abteilung 654.' (Die Deutsche Wochenschau)

'These film frames are of great interest for a genuine picture of a Bergepanther towing a Jagdpanther – and on the actual battlefield – is very rare. In the shot at the top of the page we can see the special equipment welded on the front armour plate of the Bergepanther and the German cross, and in the other shot (above) the 'Bz III' tactical number on the rear'.
(Die Deutsche Wochenschau)

The Rue de Colmar in Obenheim today, looking eastwards.

the west side of the Rhone-Rhine Canal believing that the French forces between the canal and the Rhine would simply fall back if Erstein could be taken quickly enough. This proved the case when, on January 7, one regiment of the 198. Infanterie-Division drove north with tanks and assault guns of Panzerbrigade 106 in support, and reached Erstein during the first day. It then swung back to the south-west along the Ill river to trap French units engaging the rest of the 198. Infanterie-Division. Most of the surrounded French troops managed to escape across the Ill that night and the Germans then secured the west bank of the Rhine as far as Erstein.

Operation 'Sonnenwende' formally ended there on January 13 for the continuation of the attack northwards was cancelled when the 245. Infanterie-Division that was to launch the second part of the operation was ordered to the Eastern Front. Its scheduled replacement, the 2. Gebirgs-Division, was late in arriving so, consequently, the LXIV. Armeekorps was left with an even larger perimeter to defend with fewer units.

THE COLMAR POCKET

It took much longer than General Devers had anticipated to counter the German Ardennes offensive and it was January 11 before he and de Lattre were able to meet at Vittel to discuss a renewal of operations to clear the Colmar pocket. Both were eager to launch the attack before rainfall and warmer temperatures began to melt the accumulated snowfall which would make the going extremely difficult. For the moment though, Devers felt that the 1ère Armée was too weak to carry the operation alone so he planned to obtain additional units from the SHAEF reserve.

Two days later, General Walter Bedell Smith, Eisenhower's Chief-of-Staff,

The Battle of Alsace • **249**

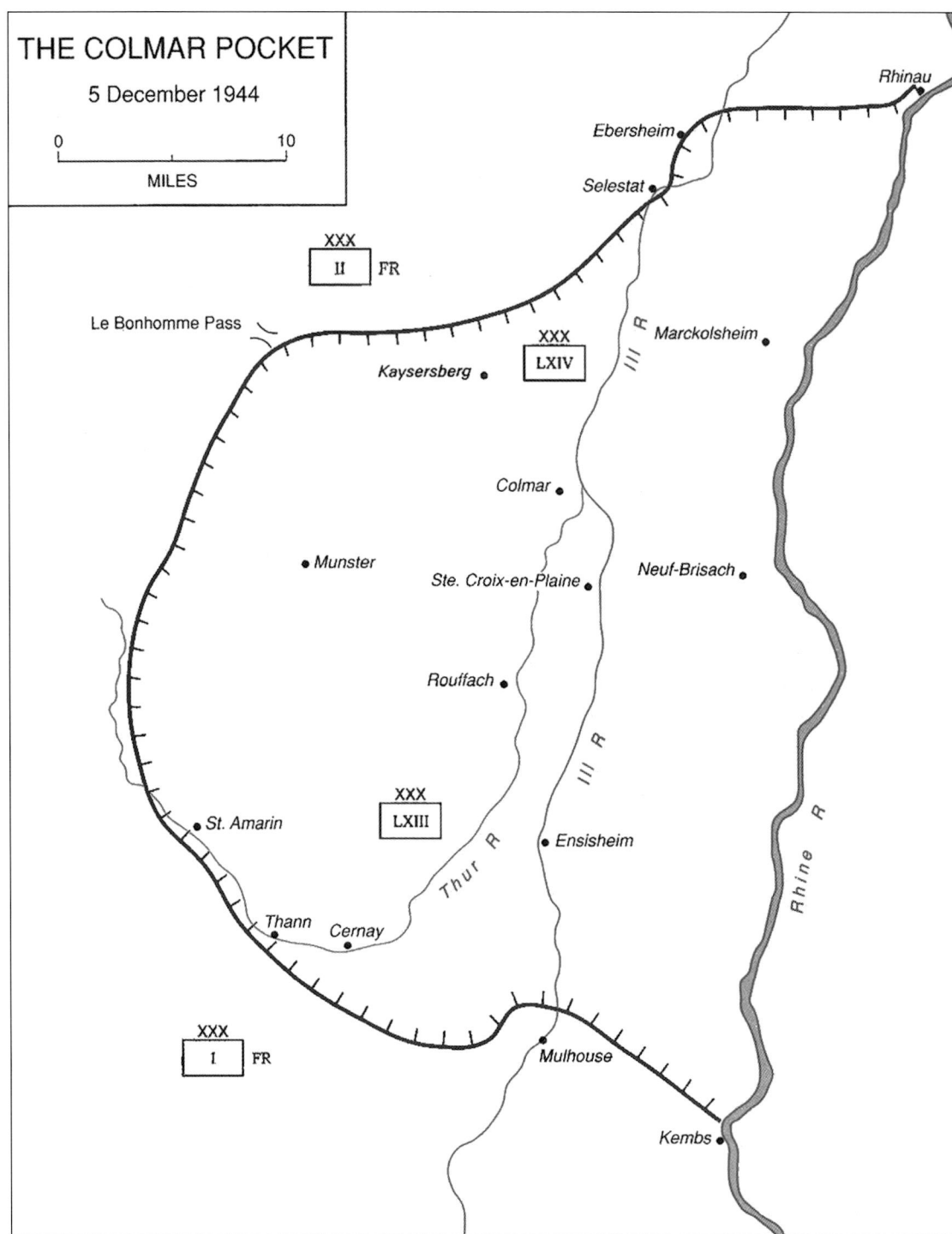

By the beginning of December, the Germans were left in possession of a large bridgehead west of the Rhine and, taking advantage of the delays caused by the re-shuffle within 6th Army Group, they were able to reorganise and strengthen this bridgehead, soon to become known in the Allied camp as the Colmar pocket.
(*Riviera to the Rhine, the US Army Official History* by Jeffrey J. Clarke and Robert Ross Smith)

The strength of the German offensive in the Ardennes on December 16 soon became clear and on the 19th December 19, Eisenhower held a conference at Verdun attended by Devers, Bradley and Patton. He directed the Third Army to turn northwards and strike against the southern shoulders of the German advance in the Ardennes. The 6th Army Group was to take over for most of the sector vacated by the Third Army. In consequence, Devers ordered the Seventh Army to adopt a defensive posture and occupy the extended front, spreading out to the west and northwest. As to the 1ère Armée, he directed it to break off the action against Colmar for the time being but to resume the offensive no later than January 5. This photo of Generals Devers and Patch was taken at the latter's headquarters in Lunéville in January 1945.
(*Riviera to the Rhine, the US Army Official History* by Jeffrey J. Clarke and Robert Ross Smith)

visited the 6th Army Group at which point Devers made his request for two divisions, an infantry division to reinforce the 3rd Division at Colmar and an armoured division to replace the 2ème Division Blindée which he intended to return south. Smith convinced Eisenhower that the request was justified and on the following day, January 14, he signalled Devers that the US 10th Armored and 28th Infantry Divisions were to be allocated to 6th Army Group. He warned him however that the 28th Division was still licking its wounds suffered in the Ardennes and was capable of only limited offensive action.

Meanwhile, the 6th Army Group planners had drawn up an operational plan for a simultaneous attack on both sides of the pocket, aiming towards the major surviving Rhine bridge near Neuf-Brisach. The Ier Corps d'Armée was to lead off in the south with a drive from Mulhouse directly to the bridge area, with a secondary attack in the Vosges north of Thann in order to tie down German forces in that area. After the German reserves had hopefully moved to the south, the US XXI Corps would then launch two infantry divisions and the 2ème Division Blindée in the direction of Neuf-Brisach, assisted perhaps by an airborne assault. Meanwhile, the IIème Corps d'Armée would seize Colmar itself. The planners estimated that the operation dubbed 'Cheerful'

The Battle of Alsace • 251

The 1ère Armée, with IIème Corps d'Armée in the north and Ier Corps d'Armée in the south, was directed to renew its offensive as soon as possible and finish the job of clearing the Colmar pocket. To this end, some American forces were transferred to Général de Lattre's command. The 3rd Infantry Division replaced the exhausted 36th Division on December 15 and the 28th Infantry Division followed from mid-January. The US XXI Corps was then transferred to the 1ère Armée to take over these two divisions plus the American 75th Division from the beginning of February. This picture was taken at Riedwihr in January when General Devers, in company with Général Henri de Vernejoul, the commander of the French 5ème Division Blindée (left), met with officers of the US 3rd Division. (ECPAD)

would take about one week and, after studying weather and flood records, they recommended that it begin in early February, certainly before the 20th.

SHAEF replied that there were no airborne forces available which did not upset Devers as he saw their employment as an unnecessary complication. However, it was the timing which disturbed him for he was worried about rising temperatures and he insisted that the operation begin earlier, even without the XXI Corps and the 2ème Division Blindée. Instead the IIème Corps d'Armée was to make the main effort against Neuf-Brisach. The concept to employ a secondary attack in the south to draw off German reserves was retained and so the plans were finalised as follows.

On the southern flank of the pocket, the Ier Corps d'Armée was to start the attack on January 20. The corps' main effort was to be on the left between Thann and Cernay, and over the Thur river toward Ensisheim, with the 4ème Division Marocaine de Montagne (DMM) and the 2ème Division d'Infanterie Marocaine (DIM) and some tanks of the 1ère Division Blindée in support. At the same time the 9ème Division d'Infanterie Coloniale (DIC)

Following the German attacks in northern Alsace, the 6th Army Group retained the 2ème Division Blindée – arguably its best armoured force – in reserve. On January 15, now confident that Seventh Army could handle the situation in northern Alsace, General Devers decided to commit more forces against the Colmar pocket itself and so ordered the French armour to move south. Light tanks in Rosheim, 25 kilometres south-west of Strasbourg. (ECPAD)

Place de la République today.

was to push into the suburbs and woods north of Mulhouse. Once these forces had cleared this territory between Cernay, Ensisheim and Mulhouse, and had secured bridges over the Ill river at Ensisheim, the main body of the 1ère Division Blindée would pass through and drive for Neuf-Brisach.

To the north, the IIème Corps d'Armée was to attack on the 22nd, two days after the beginning of the operations in the south. The 3rd Infantry Division

The Battle of Alsace • 253

A thick layer of snow had fallen during the night and down the main street this Sherman of the 501ème Régiment de Chars de Combat had not yet been cleared. (ECPAD)

Another nicely restored part of Rosheim with the gate by the Hohenbourg school barring the street, now Rue du Général de Gaulle.

in the centre, reinforced by one combat command of the 5ème Division Blindée, was to undertake the main effort, pushing south-east from the area between Sélestat and Kaysersberg. On its left, the 1ère Division de Marche d'Infanterie (DMI), with some of the 2ème Division Blindée armour attached, would push east, covering the northern flank of the attack. Once the 3rd

This series of pictures showing tanks of the 2ème Division Blindée was taken about January 20-25 when the division was assembling in the Molsheim area, west of Strasbourg, after Devers' decision to commit it against the northern flank of the German pocket in Alsace. (ECPAD)

Much of the architectural heritage in the picturesque town of Rosheim is timeless. This gate at the eastern entrance in the fortifications dates from the 14th Century.

Division had secured bridgeheads over the Colmar Canal, about halfway to the Rhine, the rest of the 5ème Division Blindée was then to be committed to seize the objective area.

Numerous streams, rivers and canals lay in the paths of advance of both corps so large amounts of bridging equipment were required. The 1ère Armée had even replaced many of the existing Bailey bridges in their area with timber structures to create extra reserves of bridging materiel, and the 6th Army Group managed to obtain a bridge company from the Third Army to provide support for the 3rd Division.

In Alsace, the 19. Armee controlled two corps headquarters situated inside the Colmar pocket comprising eight infantry divisions and one

On January 25, the 2ème Division Blindée was ordered to cross the Ill river and clear the Herbsheim-Witternheim area, 30 kilometres south of Strasbourg, in support of the 1ère Division de Marche d'Infanterie that had encountered strong resistance here. Here engineers complete the construction of a pontoon bridge across the Ill at Kogenheim, probably on the 26th. (ECPAD)

A lucky fall of snow enabled the author to take a 'seasonal' comparison.

armoured brigade. The right (northern) wing of the pocket was held by General Thumm's LXIV. Armeekorps, with the 189. and 198. Infanterie-Divisions and the 16. and 708. Volksgrenadier-Divisions. In the north, Operation 'Sonnenwende' had left the 198. Infanterie-Division holding the Erstein salient and the 708. Volksgrenadier-Division along a north-south line on the Ill river from Sélestat south to Colmar. The 189. Infanterie-Division took over in Colmar itself and the 16. Volksgrenadier-Division outposted the mountainous western section of the pocket. In the south, Generalleutnant Erich Abraham's LXIll. Armeekorps had the 338., 159. and 716. lnfanterie-Divisions. The weak 338. Infanterie-Division was in the mountains northwest of Thann, the 159. Infanterie-Division centred on Cernay and the 716. lnfanterie-Division opposite Mulhouse.

The army reserve comprised just the 269. Infanterie-Division and Panzerbrigade 106, but the former was in the process of deploying to the Eastern Front and its replacement, the 2. Gebirgs-Division, had yet to arrive.

All of these divisions were understrength and undertrained (their units had been fleshed out with hastily trained replacements and recruits). They were also under-equipped, having only about 30 to 40 per cent of their anti-tank weapons and little ammunition for their more numerous artillery pieces. Armour was even scarcer, totalling perhaps 65 operational tanks and assault guns with Panzerbrigade 106 (in army reserve), Sturmgeschütz-Brigade 280 and Panzerjäger-Abteilung 654.

On the plus side was the fact that the 19. Armee had good roads to its rear, good wire communications and ample rations and stocks of mines and small-arms ammunition. The weather and terrain also favoured the defence, as did the Alsatian network of small towns, each of which could be turned into a fortress.

Key to the 19. Armee defensive efforts in Alsace was the availability of bridges and ferries over the Rhine. Two bridges remained – at Breisach and Neuenburg; two very strong structures which had proved impossible to destroy by air attacks. In addition, the 19. Armee maintained numerous ferry sites along the river capable of handling 8-, 16- and 40-ton loads with even a few of 70-ton capacity. Near Breisach alone were four 10-ton, six 16-ton and one 70-ton ferry sites, two cable ferries and one fuel pipeline.

As scheduled, the Ier Corps d'Armée attack jumped off in the south on January 20 but the weather forecast proved wrong and the operation began in the middle of a driving snowstorm. Hitting at the boundary between the 159. and 716. Infanterie-Divisions, the French achieved tactical surprise and drove forward several kilometres on the first day but the Germans reacted quickly. A series of small counter-attacks were launched with armoured support by elements of Panzerbrigade 106 throughout the 21st which managed to retain hold of Cernay and contain the French gains above Mulhouse.

When Général Émile Béthouart, the Ier Corps d'Armée commander, shifted his main effort to the right where the 9ème Division d'Infanterie Coloniale had done better, he soon found out that the German resistance was solid right across the front. The French attacks were channelled by roads, forests, streams and small towns through a series of heavily-defended strong points organised in depth. Bypassed defenders successfully pulled back in order, aided by the heavy snowfall and overcast skies that limited Allied air support and vehicle mobility.

In the south, the Ier Corps d'Armée jumped off as scheduled on January 20 with the 4ème Division Marocaine de Montagne and the 2ème Division d'Infanterie Marocaine undertaking the main effort between Cernay and Mulhouse and the 9ème Division d'Infanterie Coloniale making another thrust north of Mulhouse. The objective was to clear a triangular shape of territory between Cernay, Ensisheim and Mulhouse and seize bridges over the Ill river at Ensisheim. Adverse weather and terrain and stubborn resistance quickly broke the tempo of the advance and it was not before the 30th that the 9ème DIC finally took Wittenheim, five kilometres north of Mulhouse. This shot of men from the 6ème Régiment d'Infanterie Coloniale in the centre of Wittenheim was taken on January 31 when the 9ème DIC completed the clearing of the town. (ECPAD)

At the end of January, after 11 days of fighting, the French were still six kilometres short of Ensisheim, their intermediate objective. By then, Béthouart reported that his infantry was exhausted, his stocks of artillery ammunition almost depleted, and two of his armoured division's three tank battalions reduced to between 16 and 18 operable armoured vehicles apiece. Combat Command 1 (CC1) alone had lost 36 tanks during the offensive to German mines.

The Ier Corps d'Armée attack in the south had at least succeeded in its

Ensisheim, the 9ème DIC intermediate objective, was still a disappointing five kilometres away. This M10 pictured in Wittenheim belonged to the 9ème Régiment de Chasseurs d'Afrique, the tank destroyer regiment of the 1ère Division Blindée, of which Combat Command 1 had been attached to the 9ème DIC to try to bolster its difficult advance. (ECPAD)

first goal, that of drawing the German armoured reserves southward, for Heeresgruppe Oberrhein had quickly approved the commitment of those parts of Panzerjäger-Abteilung 654 that were yet in reserve and also ordered Panzerbrigade 106 and the arriving elements of the 2. Gebirgs-Division to the threatened area.

In the north, the IIème Corps d'Armée attack began on January 22 as planned and initially achieved some success. Major General John E. O'Daniel, the 3rd Division commander, had planned his attack with a successive series of assaults by his four infantry regiments (the 7th, 15th and 30th and the attached 254th). Each was to push east for a few kilometres and then drive south for another 10 to 15 kilometres; the next attacking regiment would pass through the rear lines of the first and then attack east for a few kilometres before turning south as the first had done. In this way O'Daniel hoped to side-step the entire division south-east to the Colmar Canal and beyond, opening a path for a final drive on Neuf-Brisach by the 5ème Division Blindée. The manoeuvre might also deceive the Germans into believing that the Americans were trying to outflank Colmar when their real objective was the Neuf-Brisach bridge and ferry sites.

On the left, the 2ème DIM also tried hard to turn the German defences of the Cernay sector and cut them from the rear but, aided by heavy snowfalls and overcast skies that limited Allied air support, the 159. Infanterie-Division held on stubbornly. Four kilometres east of Cernay, the sector of Wittelsheim was hotly contested from January 22 and it was not before February 3 that the town was finally secured. This Sherman M4A2 of the 5ème Régiment de Chasseurs d'Afrique was part of the 1ère Division Blindée's Combat Command 2 that was attached to the 2ème DIM. (ECPAD)

The picture was taken in the Cité Graffenwald by the side of the D19 two kilometres south of Wittelsheim. When the author first pinpointed the location in the spring of 2002 the tree which appears off to the right in the 1945 photo was still there but by the time he returned to match up the shot the following winter, it had been felled.

On the evening of February 3, the gap left open between the Ier Corps d'Armée near Ensisheim and the XXI Corps near Sainte-Croix-en-Plaine was down to 15 kilometres. The Germans then speeded up their withdrawal from the Vosges and abandoned Cernay during that night. As the 4ème Division de Montagne Marocaine entered the town the following morning, the stunned inhabitants emerged from their cellars to discover the street littered with tree branches cut off by shrapnel intermingled with the bodies of dead German soldiers. (ECPAD)

Cernay, Rue Poincaré today.

General Thumm, the LXIV. Armeekorps commander, had noted the Allied build-up between Colmar and Sélestat and had directed the 708. Volksgrenadier-Division to maintain only a thin defensive screen west of the Ill river, keeping enough forces to the rear for strong local counter-attacks. To add some strength, he had attached Sturmgeschütz-Brigade 280 with some tanks and assault guns to the division.

At first, all on the Allied side went according to plan. The 7th Infantry Regiment crossed the Fecht river at Guémar (which was already in Allied hands) late on January 22 and proceeded south. Following them, the 30th Infantry crossed the river during the night of January 22/23 and started to

As the 6ème Régiment de Tirailleurs Marocains cleared Cernay and rounded up prisoners, the rest of the 4ème DMM pressed northwards. Brushing aside scattered German forces trying to withdraw from the Vosges, the leading French troops reached Rouffach in the evening. The surprised Germans reacted quickly; consequently, the small French force had to withdraw for the night into the southern outskirts of the town. (ECPAD)

enter the Colmar forest through deep snow. The unit's initial objective was the Maison Rouge bridge, a wooden span over the Ill opposite the south-eastern corner of the forest and Colonel Lionel C. McGarr, the regimental commander, split his force into two attacking forces. The 3rd Battalion was to head south-east directly for the bridge while the 1st Battalion struck out eastwards to cross the Ill about a mile or so above the bridge and move down to the crossing site from the north. The 1st Battalion managed to cross the Ill in rubber boats during the night unopposed and sweep down the east bank of the river, surprising a small detachment of Germans at the bridge. When day dawned on January 23, the 30th Infantry was in possession of the Ill bridge as well as the cross-roads to the east and the farm complex of Maison Rouge in between.

The bridgehead was consolidated in the early morning hours of the 24th whereupon patrols were pushed out to the east, south-east and south. With the Germans apparently failing to react, McGarr decided to continue the advance to Riedwihr and Holtzwihr, the intermediate regimental objectives. He directed the 1st Battalion to move through the woods toward Riedwihr; the 3rd Battalion to pass behind the 1st and advance on Holtzwihr, some

In the north, the IIème Corps d'Armée attacked late on January 22 when the 7th and 30th Infantry Regiments crossed the Fecht river at Guémar and swept southwards during the night. On the following day, as the leading elements of the 30th Infantry took the Maison Rouge bridge across the Ill, on the right the 7th Infantry cleared the village of Ostheim. A French photographer, Henri Malin, took this picture some days later when the 254th Infantry Regiment (attached to the US 3rd Division) passed through Ostheim on their way eastwards to the Jebsheim sector. (ECPAD)

Only one of the original houses, the one on the left, remains on the present-day Rue de Strasbourg.

Combat Command 6 of the French 5ème Division Blindée also passed through Ostheim on their way to Jebsheim. (ECPAD)

The Protestant church in the town had been so badly damaged that it had to be rebuilt on a new site on the bank of the Fecht river. This is actually the far end of the Rue de Strasbourg which runs to the left at this junction.

distance farther south; and the 2nd to follow the 1st into the Riedwihr woods as a reserve.

Just before midday, the leading elements of the 1st Battalion reported hearing enemy armour around Riedwihr and later, from the eastern edge of the woods, they reported seeing a few German armoured vehicles proceeding through the town. McGarr became increasingly nervous about his lack of armoured support east of the river so he pushed for engineer assistance with reinforcing the bridge at Maison Rouge which had been taken intact but was not strong enough to support tanks. One Sherman of the attached tank company was run up and down the west ramp, causing the structure to shake and sway so violently that it ended any ideas the tankers might have had of charging across. It was decided to strengthen the centre spans and reinforce the surface with treadway bridging but when the sections finally arrived around 3 p.m., there were too few to cover the whole length of the bridge and approach ramps.

Pressed by O'Daniel, who called him again at 3.55 p.m., McGarr was

This picture captioned 'in the Riedwihr area' slots perfectly into our story at this point because it shows one of the treadway bridges established over the Ill river although it does not say that this is the actual Maison Rouge bridge. Taken on February 1, this shot features men of the US 75th Division moving in for the final push to Colmar. (USNA)

ordered to begin the attack on Riedwihr and Holtzwihr at 4.30 p.m. The 1st Battalion met heavy enemy fire as it approached Riedwihr and was barely able to reach the outskirts of town. The 3rd Battalion moved into Holtzwihr but was counter-attacked by strong tank/infantry teams. Both units requested immediate assistance to deal with the enemy armour.

Under pressure to bring at least some tanks across the bridge at once, the engineers choose to use the available treadway sections to overlay the two unsteady ramps in the hope that the shorter centre spans would support the

This is the bridge at Maison Rouge as it appears today, looking eastwards. Lieutenant John F. Harmon drove his Sherman up the western ramp – just as these cyclists are doing – but when the tank reached the centre span, the bridge collapsed and the tank fell into the river.

The Battle of Alsace • 265

Pushing south from Maison Rouge, the 15th Infantry took Riedwihr on January 26 but met strong resistance as they tried to advance to the Colmar Canal. (ECPAD)

This is the southern entrance of Riedwihr joining the road from Wickerschwihr.

weight. After running three 57mm anti-tank guns and their movers and a large ten-ton truck across the bridge, at 5 p.m. Lieutenant John F. Harmon drove his Sherman up the reinforced ramp and onto the centre span. As soon as the tank had cleared the reinforcing treadway section and driven onto the centre section, the bridge gave way and the tank fell into the river. No more vehicles would cross the Ill river for many hours.

All three battalions east of the river then suddenly found themselves in the midst of a general counter-attack by elements of the 708. Volksgrenadier-Division and Sturmgeschütz-Brigade 280. Around 6 p.m. one American tank officer who had crossed the Maison Rouge bridge on foot to reconnoitre the opposite side, reported streams of soldiers pouring back from the Riedwihr woods in complete disorder, abandoning weapons and attempting to climb over the damaged bridge. In the words of the official US Army historians Clarke and Smith: 'In the background he noted white tracers from German automatic weapons mingled with the red tracers of American arms – someone was still fighting – but most of the regiment appeared to be taking refuge along the stream and riverbanks or braving the cold waters of the Ill to reach the opposite shore. There, frustrated tank and tank destroyer crews watched the debacle and shortly thereafter, as the sunlight began to fade, they spotted the squat German assault guns moving up two by two, each section covering the advance of the other. Anti-tank and artillery fire kept the counter-attacking force at bay for a while, but sometime after dark the bridgehead appeared to be in German hands, though no one could tell for sure.'

At 8.30 p.m. O'Daniel ordered Lieutenant Colonel Hallett D. Edson, the commander of the 15th Infantry, to secure the bridgehead, see to the repair of the structure, and resume the 3rd Division's attack as soon as possible. Edson alerted his 3rd Battalion and immediately sent two of its rifle companies, I and K, to cross the Ill some distance above the bridge. Descending on Maison Rouge from the north as the 30th Infantry's 1st Battalion had done 24 hours earlier, at 5 a.m. on the 24th the two companies scattered the small German holding force at the bridge and rescued a number of 30th Regiment infantrymen who had somehow survived the night on the east bank.

Clarke and Smith: 'Instructed to defend both the bridge area and the cross-roads, the battalion commander gave Company K the responsibility for the crossing site and sent Company I out to occupy the cross-roads. As dawn came, the Company I commander, finding the cross-roads completely exposed and without any cover, requested permission to pull the unit back to the tree line, but was instructed to hold in place: division engineers were just completing a new treadway bridge to the north and armoured support could be expected shortly. For the next several hours the men of Company I frantically chipped away at the frozen ground, digging up at best a few inches of dirt, ice and snow and wondering when the tanks would arrive. They finally came about three hours later, but from the wrong side.

'At 8 a.m. on the 24th, the Germans launched their second counter-

Two battalions of the 30th Infantry then moved through the 15th Infantry and resumed the attack south of Riedwhir on January 27 with Combat Command 4 of the 5ème Division Blindée in support. Holtzwihr and Wickerschwihr were captured and the Colmar canal was reached. Later a French photographer, Fernand Charleuf, pictured a Jagdpanther from Panzerjäger-Abteilung 654 abandoned at Wickerschwihr. This was a late-production model with the heavy bolted gun mantle. (ECPAD)

The two houses visible in the background of the photo gave the author the clue for pinpointing the particular field between Wickerschwihr and Holtzwihr where the Jagdpanther met its end.

attack against the bridgehead with 13 heavy assault guns and a company or more of infantry. As the enemy machines began pushing through the mile or so of fields between Company I and the Riedwihr woods, the American soldiers scrambled into their makeshift foxholes and watched and waited, lying flat on the frozen ground. Friendly artillery soon caused the attacking infantry, barely visible at first, to disperse and lag behind; but the assault guns, accompanied by a few tanks and lighter armoured vehicles, continued toward them at a steady pace. The company commander and his forward observer ticked off the German progress for many to hear – 800 yards away, then 600 and then 500. A few panicked and fled and others asked their officers; "Can we go?" The rest stayed, although, as one sergeant later

In the meantime, a few kilometres to the north-east, the 254th Infantry and Combat Command 6 attacked Jebsheim where violent fighting continued throughout the 27th and the 28th. By the evening the village was at last firmly in Allied hands. (ECPAD)

This 75mm anti-tank gun abandoned by the side of the road leading from Jebsheim to the canal south of the village was one of those which, together with the deadly 88mm guns of some Nashorn tank destroyers of Panzerjäger-Abteilung 525, destroyed three Sherman tanks and three M10 tank destroyers of the French command during the fighting for the village. (ECPAD)

The Germans fought hard to retain Jebsheim and their losses were heavy and at least 800 prisoners were reported to have been taken by the Franco-American force. When Henri Malin took these pictures on January 29 the Germans were already preparing their counter-attack. (ECPAD)

recalled "we all practically had one foot out of the foxhole" and when the company commander finally made the decision to pull back "we didn't have to give the order very loud".

'That morning, shortly after 8 a.m., the company was overrun. Some soldiers were crushed under the German tank treads or machine-gunned where they lay; others managed to fall back into the Company K area closer to the river; still others were shot while trying to surrender.'

The battle for the bridgehead continued throughout the morning and into the early afternoon, neither side being able to secure the area. While direct fire from American tanks and tank destroyers from across the Ill river had forced the German assault guns back, the German infantrymen were unable to overcome the American defenders. Two American tanks and a tank destroyer finally crossed the new treadway bridge established some distance to the north and charged south only to be promptly disabled by German assault guns. Finally, about 2.30 p.m., the 1st Battalion of the 15th Infantry counter-attacked from the north with more armour in support and managed to relieve the men trapped at the bridge.

The 15th Infantry continued its advance southwards and entered Riedwihr on the night of January 25/26. For two days, the Germans launched repeated

Elements of Gebirgsjäger-Regiment 136 with some Jagdpanthers of Panzerjäger-Abteilung 654 in support mounted the attack on Jebsheim on the morning of the 29th and again in that afternoon. That same day, Malin took this shot of American infantry resuming the advance from Jebsheim eastwards in the direction of Artzenheim. (ECPAD)

No snow and a much nicer weather when the author took this comparison in February 2003.

Although this is another Jagdpanther disabled near Jebsheim – one of the five lost in the sector during the last days of January – it is important to stress that the Germans did not possess strong armoured forces in Alsace. By mid-January, with the 30 Jagdpanthers of Panzerjäger-Abteilung 654 and the armour available to Sturmgeschütz-Brigade 280 and Panzerbrigade 106, there were no more than 55 panzers of various types available. (ECPAD)

It was January 31 when Malin took this last shot. The snow had melted over the previous two days, turning the street into a sea of mud. (ECPAD)

A café has since replaced the station inn named the Gasthaus zum Bahnhof, which once occupied this corner of Jebsheim.

counter-attacks with no success. It was during one of these attempts on the 26th that 2nd Lieutenant Audie Murphy earned the Medal of Honor for turning back several attacks from the turret of a burning tank destroyer. The Colmar Canal was crossed on the night of January 29/30 and the following day the 3rd Division's three regiments drove several kilometres south of the canal to secure the crossing sites. The advance then halted. The 3rd Division was exhausted, with some of its rifle companies down to 30 men.

General Devers then decided to commit the XXI Corps to control three American divisions, the 3rd, the 28th and the 75th Infantry Divisions, for a drive on Neuf-Brisach, with the US 12th Armored Division (still recovering from a catastrophic commitment at Herrlisheim) in reserve. De Lattre concurred and also agreed to assign the

This is Rue Kléber; Place Rapp lies just behind the photographer.

At 7 a.m. on February 3 the US XXI Corps launched the final push into Colmar. The 109th Infantry led the advance, followed by a battle group of the 5ème Division Blindée. Here an M5 light tank of the 1er Régiment de Cuirassiers rounds the corner as crowds line the street to cheer their liberators. (USNA)

The Battle of Alsace • **273**

AUDIE MURPHY'S MEDAL OF HONOR

On 25 January, engineers erected a bridge over the Ill north of Maison Rouge and over the next two days the 15th Infantry pushed south toward Riedwihr and Holtzwihr. On the 26th a German force of infantry and tanks moving from Holtzwihr attacked Company B near the Riedwihr Woods. The Germans scored a direct hit on an M10 tank destroyer, forcing the crew to abandon it, and Lieutenant Murphy ordered his men to retreat to positions in the woods. He remained alone at his post and directed artillery fire via his field radio.

1st Lieutenant Walter W. Weispfenning, a Field Artillery forward observer, described Murphy's stand in the official history of the 3rd Division:

'While we tried to hold off the tanks with directed artillery fire and bazooka rockets, the German infantry line, consisting of two full strength companies of 125 men each, surged across the open meadow in a wide arc.

'Then I saw Lieutenant Murphy do the bravest thing that I have ever seen a man do in combat. With the Germans only a hundred yards away and still moving up on him, he climbed into the slowly-burning tank destroyer and began firing the .50-calibre machine gun at the krauts. He was completely exposed and silhouetted against the background of bare trees and snow, with a fire under him that threatened to blow the destroyer to bits if it reached the gasoline and ammunition. Eighty-eight millimetre shells, machine-gun, machine-pistol and rifle fire crashed all about him.

'Standing on top of the tank destroyer, Murphy raked the approaching enemy force with machine gun fire. Twelve Germans, stealing up a ditch to flank him from his right, were killed in the gully at 50-yard range by concentrated fire from his machine gun. Twice the tank destroyer he was standing on was hit by artillery fire and the Lieutenant was enveloped in clouds of smoke and spurts of flame. His clothing was torn and riddled by flying shell fragments and bits of rock. Bullets ricocheted off the tank destroyer as the enemy concentrated the full fury of his fire on this one-man strongpoint.'

In 1958, Murphy agreed to play himself in a film based on the 1949 autobiography about his wartime exploits *To Hell and Back*. This is the action which won Murphy the congressional Medal of Honor as depicted in the film. Note that a Sherman tank was used in the film whereas a M10 tank destroyer was the actual vehicle at Holtzwihr. (Universal)

After the Battle artist George Campbell painted this remarkable rendering of the Medal of Honor scene at Holtzwihr.

Unable to determine where the machine-gun was firing from, the German force first became confused and finally retreated back to Holtzwihr.

Murphy sustained a leg wound during his stand but he finally led his company in to dislodge the Germans from the whole area. When the fight was over, he allowed his wound to be treated on the field. Riedwihr fell to the 15th Infantry on January 26, and Holtzwihr was taken by the 30th Infantry on the 27th.

For his actions that day, Murphy was awarded the Medal of Honor.

The exploits of Audie Murphy at Holtzwihr was one of the first stories researched by Winston Ramsey when he created *After the Battle* magazine and the story appeared in issue No. 3 in 1973. He researched the battle field with his friend Roger Bell who stands in this photo on the spot where the M10 tank destroyer was disabled in 1945. Winston reported: 'The ditch where the Germans were shot is on the right. The scarred tree remains, beneath which the machine gun squad were killed by a tree burst. The forest is now much thicker than it was, with new saplings and underbrush, but the stumps of the old trees remain.' Indications are that the TD had blown up, and was pushed off the road some time after the battle.

General Mike O'Daniel, Commander of the 3rd Infantry Division, personally congratulates Lieutenant Murphy and shows him the Congressional Medal of Honor, which General Patch will shortly award him. (Associated Press)

Lieutenant Murphy after the ceremony held on an airstrip at Salzburg, Austria on June 2, 1945. In addition to the Medal of Honor, he had the Legion of Merit pinned on his breast (awarded for fighting in Germany on February 18, 1945). (Keystone)

Under contract with Universal, Murphy became one of their top Western stars and made more than 40 films. He was under no illusions however and once said he had made the same Western 30 times with different horses. He was relatively inactive as an actor after the late 1960s. On May 28, 1971, he was on a private flight from Atlanta, Georgia, to Martinsville, Virginia when the plane was reported missing. The next day the wrecked plane – an Aero Commander twin-engine aircraft registered as N601JJ – was found 15 miles north-west of Roanoke, having crashed on Brush Mountain in the Allegheny range. The collision into the heavily wooded slope and ensuing fire destroyed the plane and all six people were dead. Murphy and two other passengers had been thrown uphill from the wreckage but the other three were found within the cabin and were badly burned. The National Transportation Safety Board concluded that the crash was caused by the pilot's decision to continue visual flight into adverse weather conditions. (Associated Press)

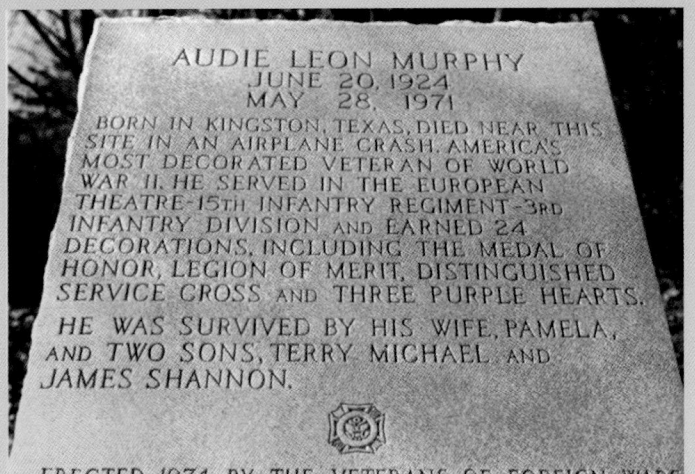

The memorial stone which now marks the spot of his death.

On June 7, 1971, Audie Murphy was buried, with full military honours including a 21-gun salute, in Arlington National Cemetery, Washington, in front of the tomb of the Unknown Soldier. Sergeant First Class William Rosenmund of the Signal Support Unit took this photo. (USNA)

Audie Murphy's grave today in Arlington National Cemetery. In addition to the Medal of Honor, he was awarded the Bronze Star for his actions in Italy on March 2, 1944; the Distinguished Service Cross for the battle at Ramatuelle on August 15, 1944; the Silver Star for feats in the Vosges on October 2, 1944 and the Legion of Merit for fighting in Germany on February 18, 1945. He also had four Purple Hearts, an additional Bronze and Silver Star and the European Theater Medal with seven Battle Stars, the French Légion d'Honneur and the French Croix de Guerre. (Arlington National Cemetery)

The Battle of Alsace • 277

Marty Black, a long time American reader and fan of *After the Battle*, visited the site of Audie Murphy's Holtzwihr action in the late 1990s and found that the old battle-scarred tree (see George Campbell's painting and Winston Ramsey's photo from 1973) was gone, and that the 'butt end of the U' of the woods line (as Audie Murphy described it in To Hell and Back) had been extended south by seven rows of newly planted trees. At the edge of the old part of the woods, close to where the battle-scarred tree had been, Marty located the remains of a machine gun emplacement filled with spent .30 calibre casings, as well as several complete cartridges, the lid handle from a .30 cal ammo can and some pieces of field equipment carried by the GIs. In and around the machine gun hole were several yards of GI field telephone wire, most of which was held fast to the ground by roots.

A few metres further into the woods Marty found spent .50 cal machine gun cases and then more and more pieces of what appeared to be blown-up TD: gears, sprockets, rubber hoses, a fuel line, levers and valves, an exhaust pipe, and pieces of rubber track cleats. There were a few pieces of armour plate, the metal cover from a blackout tail light (cat's eye), the base from the whip antenna, something that looked like a horn, and various pieces of metal rod, which Marty assumed to be from the luggage rack of an armoured vehicle. The base mount for the antenna and a piece of armoured plate still had some of the olive-drab paint on them.

Scattered among this debris, and a few yards further into the trees, were many .50 calibre machine gun cases, as well as numerous corroded steel links. Most had been fired while a few had exploded under the effect of heat. Marty carefully examined the headstamps of them and found that they were from two manufacturers: Lake City 1943 and Saint Louis 1943. Marty remarked that this matched with Audie Murphy indicating in To Hell and Back that he had to open up another box of ammunition to reload the TD's machine gun at least once during his one-man-stand. The first one came from one manufacturer, the second from the other.

whole of the 5ème Division Blindée to the XXI Corps. The corps commander, Major General Frank W. Milburn, decided to continue using the 3rd Division to spearhead the attack with most of the 5ème Division Blindée to back up the tired American regiments. On the left wing, the IIème Corps d'Armée was to secure the northern flank.

As early as January 25, Heeresgruppe G had concluded that holding the Colmar pocket was no longer important to the German defensive effort in the West and recommended that either the entire pocket should be abandoned or, at least, the northern extension at Erstein be evacuated and the forces used to strengthen the northern shoulder. On the night of January 28/29 Hitler finally agreed to the partial withdrawal in the north but still insisted that the pocket be defended as long as possible.

On January 29, Heeresgruppe Oberrhein was dissolved and SS-Oberstgruppenführer Paul Hausser took command of Heeresgruppe G, including all forces formerly assigned to Heeresgruppe Oberrhein. Reichsführer-SS Himmler was reassigned to a command on the Eastern Front (Heeresgruppe Weichsel commanding three armies on the Vistula front) and Generaloberst Blaskowitz, who had commanded Heeresgruppe G from December 22, was made commander of Heeresgruppe H in Holland.

At 11.30 a.m. the leading tanks reached Place Rapp which lies in the centre of Colmar. Exhilarated tankers of the 5ème Division Blindée rejoice in the historic moment: Colmar, second only in importance to Strasbourg in the province annexed by Germany, was back in French hands. The campaign in Alsace was about to reach its finale. (ECPAD)

An M10 of the 11ème Régiment de Chasseurs d'Afrique, the tank destroyer regiment of the 5ème Division Blindée, stands guard in front of former German barracks. (USNA)

This is the main entrance to Quartier Bruat on Route de Strasbourg. The sports ground indicated by the German sign is still there bearing its original name: Stade des Francs.

The odd pockets of resistance in the city and the suburbs were progressively being cleared and at 4 p.m. the French battle group reported having taken 250 prisoners. Some 25 of them are seen here being marched up the Avenue de la République. (ECPAD)

Another time . . . but the same place! A low-lying winter sun gives superb light for our comparison in February 2003.

The Battle of Alsace • **281**

More Nazi propaganda, the message on the left claiming that 'Bolshevists and democrats are the accomplices of Jewry for the enslavement of peoples. That is why National Socialism fights unyieldingly for German liberty'. (ECPAD)

From Schlumbergerstrasse . . . to Rue Camille Schlumberger . . . Colmar . . . then . . . and now.

On February 8, a victory parade took place in Colmar when Général de Lattre de Tassigny of the 1ère Armée made his official entry in the liberated city. Here honour guards of the 12th Armored Division (forefront) and the 28th Infantry Division (in the background) give acte de présence on the main square, the Place Rapp. (USNA)

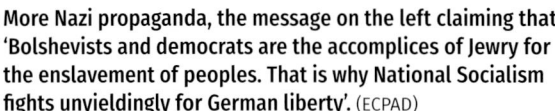

Another celebration was held in the city on February 20 when Général de Lattre awarded 57 of the highest French decorations to American commanders. Among them were Major General John E. Dahlquist of the 36th Infantry Division, Major General John E. O'Daniel of the 3rd Infantry Division and Major General Roderick C. Allen of the 12th Armored Division. (USNA)

CLEARING THE WEST BANK OF THE RHINE

German intelligence in Alsace was faulty and it was only on January 30, when the 3rd Division had crossed the Colmar Canal, that the German command began to perceive that the Allied drive was headed directly for the bridge at Neuf-Brisach. On the night of the 30th, Heeresgruppe G specified to General Rasp of 19. Armee that his main mission was to 'assure the survival' of the pocket for as long as possible. He was authorised to withdraw most of his forces from the Vosges front, leaving only reconnaissance detachments to hold the mountain passes. Rasp in turn ordered the immediate evacuation of all forces in the Vosges and concentrated them on the northern and southern shoulders of the bridgehead, while sending what reinforcement he could to protect his two major bridge sites at Breisach and Neuenburg.

Inside the pocket, the situation was soon becoming confused with elements from the 16. Volksgrenadier-Division and the 189. and 338. Infanterie-Divisions mixed with those of the other divisions as well as with units of the 2. Gebirgs-Division which had begun arriving in the

The US 12th Armored Division took over the advance southwards and in the early hours of February 5, its Combat Command A entered Rouffach. Here an M5 light tank has pulled up on the Place de la République. (USNA)

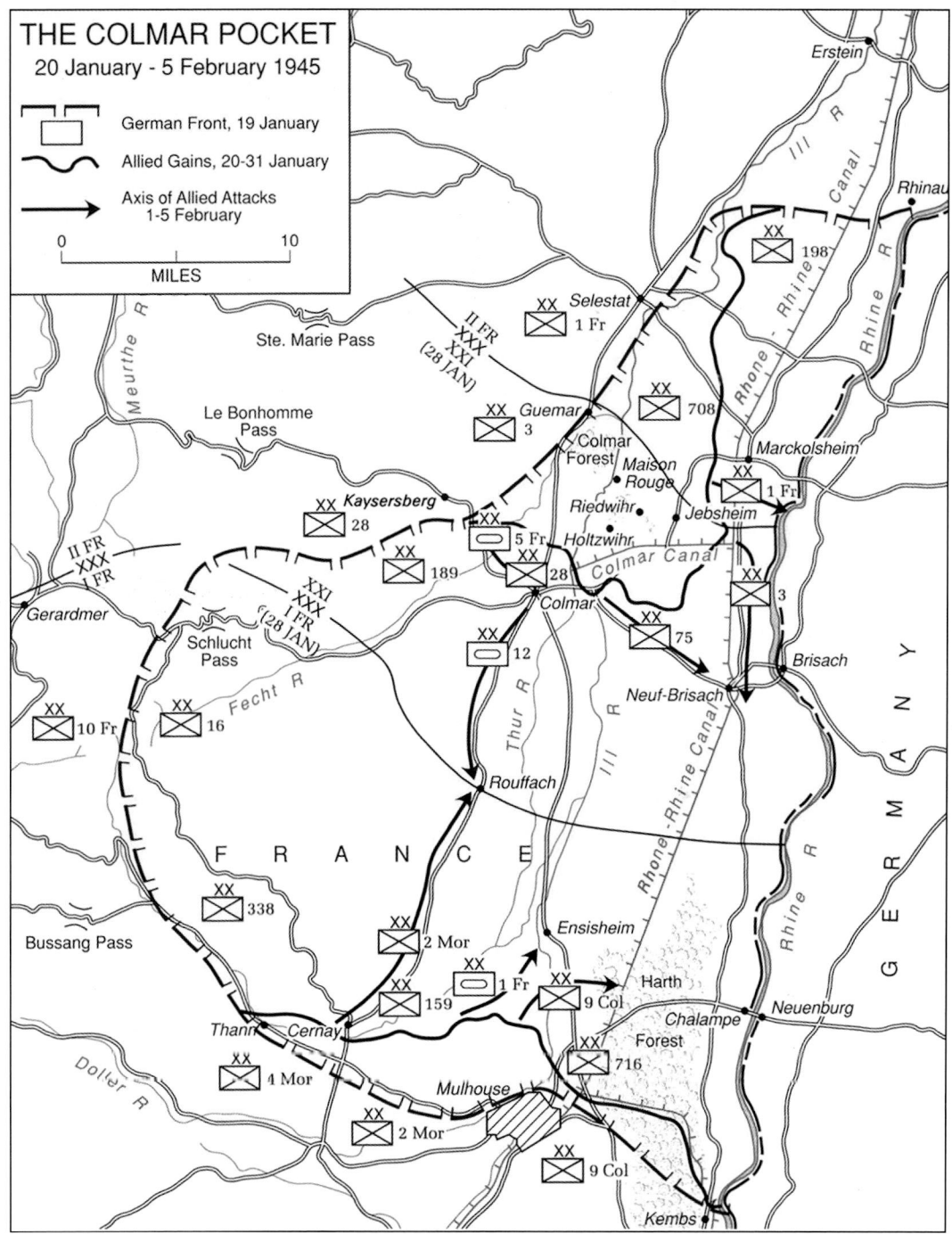

Clearing the Colmar pocket, January 20 – February 5, a map from *Riviera to the Rhine, the US Army Official History* by Jeffrey J. Clarke and Robert Ross Smith.

In Rouffach, two French soldiers, probably from the 1er Régiment de Tirailleurs Marocains, fill the hands of American soldiers of the 999th Field Artillery Battalion with candy. (USNA)

pocket sometime after the 20th. On February 1, in spite of standing orders to the contrary, General Rasp begun to move service troops and damaged equipment east of the Rhine. That evening Hitler's order to stand fast in the pocket arrived at Heeresgruppe G and was immediately passed on to Rasp by telephone. While these instructions remained unaltered to the end, from the 6th Rasp started to evacuate equipment over the Rhine by ferry or over the Neuenburg bridge while the bulk of the combat forces fell back on this same bridge.

'The 75th Infantry Division had begun moving into the 1ère Armée area on January 27', wrote the official US Army historians, 'and by the evening of the 31st started to relieve O'Daniel's 3rd Division regiments south of the Colmar Canal for the final push. Again O'Daniel attacked east and then south, first slipping the 30th Infantry behind the others and moving it east to the Rhône-Rhine Canal for a drive south with units of the 5ème Division Blindée. Next, with the arrival of the 75th Division on the battlefield, he

German pockets of resistance still held out in many places and it was not until 8 a.m., after two hours of disorganised fighting, that Rouffach was finally cleared by CCA and elements of the 4ème Division de Montagne Marocaine that had entered the town from the south. This lone prisoner surrendered to men of the 4ème Régiment de Spahis Marocains. (USNA)

This is Rue du Maréchal Joffre. Rue Poincaré lies behind the photographer.

A battle group of the 1ère Division Blindée then reached Rouffach from the south but when its commander, Chef d'Escadron de Bertereche de Menditte (left), met Brigadier General Riley F. Ennis (right) commanding CCA of the 12th Armored Division, Ennis pointed out that Rouffach lay within the XXI Corps sector of action and therefore asked that the French combat command be moved beyond the boundary. The French commander concurred and issued orders to resume the advance east using another route more to the south which ran through Munwiller. (USNA)

transferred both the 7th and 15th Infantry to the far side of the Rhône-Rhine Canal, turning them south as well. By February 3 elements of all three 3rd Division regiments were approaching Neuf-Brisach and the Germans began a last-ditch defence of the bridgehead with all available manpower. On the 5th, with the old fortress town nearly surrounded, the Germans started to evacuate the area and by noon of the following day, February 6, the entire sector was under Allied control.

'Inside the pocket the German defences around the city of Colmar had already collapsed. While the 3rd Division attacked toward Neuf-Brisach, first the attached 254th Infantry and then the regiments of the 28th Division (Major General Norman D. Cota) steadily pushed against the northern approaches to Colmar in the Kaysersberg valley. By February 2 Cota's units had cleared the city's suburbs against diminishing resistance, allowing units of the 5ème Division Blindée to drive into the heart of Colmar nearly unopposed. Immediately de Lattre agreed to commit the 12th Armored

Meanwhile GIs of the 12th Armored Division grabbed the opportunity of the lull in the fighting to catch up with their mail. From the windows of their convent, nuns observe the joyful demonstrations at the liberation of their town. (USNA)

Time has stood still at the junction between the Rue Poincaré on the right and the Rue Ris (left).

The Battle of Alsace • 289

Pushing from the south, Combat Command 3 of the 1ère Division Blindée cleared the western bank of the River Ill as far as Sainte-Croix-en-Plaine which lies some eight kilometres north-east of Rouffach and well to the north in the American sector. This picture of French troopers from CC3 was taken on February 3. (ECPAD)

Indicating that Colmar lies 17 kilometres away and Mulhouse 20 kilometres in the opposite direction, the road sign provided an easy guide to the location of the photograph: Meyenheim. This is the Grande Rue in front of the new town hall.

Combat Command B of the 12th Armored Division was late in reaching its allocated sector along the west bank of the Ill river and it was not until the morning of February 6 that all of Combat Command 3 had fulfilled its promise to move back behind the US XXI Corps boundary which had been established due east of Rouffach. (ECPAD)

After a long search, the author found that the picture of infantry dismounting from a tank had been taken on the Rue de la Gare in Meyenheim.

Division through the 28th Division for a drive south; two days later American armoured task forces, moving south along two parallel axes, met Ier Corps d'Armée elements at Rouffach during the early morning hours of February 5. By that date the bulk of Béthouart's southern forces had finally bypassed German emplacements around Ensisheim and, finding enemy defences crumbling elsewhere, raced to Rouffach from the south. The drives split the Colmar pocket wide open. Between February 5 and 9, as the supporting American divisions redeployed northward, French forces finished cleaning

The Battle of Alsace • 291

However, the tanks of the 1ère Division Blindée were held up from crossing the Ill until pontoon bridges had been constructed and it was February 7 before the first tanks of Combat Command 3 managed to get across. This is Prague, a Sherman M4A4 of the 2ème Régiment de Chasseurs d'Afrique. (ECPAD)

The author discovered that this particular bridge had been built at Meyenheim. Today its permanent replacement taking the D3bis over the river lies just behind the photographer.

out the pocket. In the north de Monsabert's forces (Général de Montsabert, the commander of IIème Corps d'Armée) swept the west side of the Rhine from Erstein to Marckolsheim, while in the west units of the new 10ème Division d'Infanterie and the 4ème Division de Montaigne Marocaine policed up the interior of the pocket.

'To the south, Béthouart directed his main effort against the last German bridgehead at Chalampé, using the 1ère Division Blindée and the 2ème Division d'Infanterie Marocaine and 9ème Division d'Infanterie Coloniale. Here German resistance remained fierce for a few days, but the French managed to penetrate across the Ill river on February 5, secure Ensisheim on the 6th and reach the Rhône-Rhine Canal by the 7th. There they were joined by Leclerc's armour on the 8th; the next morning, elements of the

In the meantime, in the north, the XXI Corps had crossed the Colmar Canal and pushed south-eastwards in the direction of Neuf-Brisach. The 75th Infantry Division had joined the operation from January 30 and the French 2ème Division Blindée from February 4, the latter taking over from the combat commands of the 5ème Division Blindée which then assembled at Colmar as 1ère Armée reserve. On February 5, while the 291st Infantry took Wolfgantzen, two kilometres north-west of Neuf-Brisach, the 289th Infantry secured Appenwihr, six kilometres to the west. A combat command of the 2ème Division Blindée then sped south through Hettenschlag to reach Dessenheim, five kilometres south of Neuf-Brisach. Late on February 5, the troops of the 15th Infantry reached the western ends of the road and rail bridges at Neuf-Brisach, both already blown up by the Germans. This Wirbelwind, a Flak tank mounting a quadruple 2cm AA gun on a PzKpfw IV chassis, had been abandoned at Hettenschlag, its crew probably taken by surprise at the sudden appearance of French tanks on the afternoon of February 5. (USNA)

A timeless comparison, the church having been untouched for the past 60 years.

The Battle of Alsace • **293**

Pressing on south-westwards, the 2ème Division Blindée took Balgau, 12 kilometres north of Chalampé, on the afternoon of the 7th. The sign at this elaborate road-block set up at the western entrance of the town announced: 'Death to the destroyers of Europe'. (USNA)

Could this really be the same place 60 years on?

9ème DIC reached the Rhine at Chalampé, forcing the Germans to destroy the remaining bridge at 8 a.m. This final act marked the end of the Colmar pocket and the German presence in upper Alsace as well.'

Hitler's decision to hold the pocket as long as possible, mainly for political reasons and probably personal esteem, had resulted in high losses for the 19. Armee. Precise German casualty reports are sparse, but it is estimated that thousands of men had been killed or wounded in Alsace. Non-combat casualties from the weather had also been high as the men had had to endure deep snow and freezing temperatures. One Heeresgruppe G report put the

The Germans destroyed the last Rhine bridge – the one between Chalampé and Neuenburg – at 8 a.m. on February 9. The forces of the Ier Corps d'Armée fighting to clear the shrinking German bridgehead heard the explosion and realised what had happened. At 11.30 a.m. the leading troops of the 9ème DIC reached the town just as the last Germans crossed the Rhine in small boats. Another propaganda message, this one claiming that when 'Stalin, Churchill and Roosevelt demolish, Hitler builds up!'. (ECPAD)

The same wall survives at Bantzenheim, two kilometres west of Chalampé.

The demolition of the last bridge across the Rhine was the final act in the battle for Alsace (also referred to in the history books as the Battle of the Colmar Pocket), and the 1ère Armée announced that the campaign officially ended at 8 a.m. on February 9. This picture of the wrecked railway bridge at Breisach was taken that same day as white phosphorous shells explode on pillboxes on the German bank of the Rhine. Having survived massive Allied bombing, it appears that German soldiers awarded this particular bridge an honorary Iron Cross! (USNA)

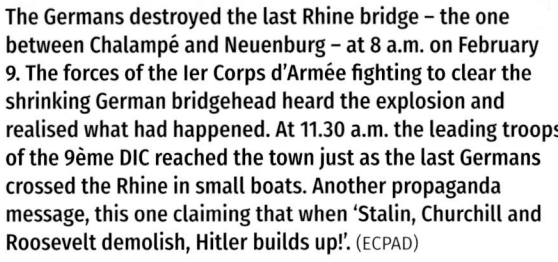

The Battle of Alsace • 295

On February 3, Signal Corps photographer T/5 Joseph A. Bowen pictured these 'Yank infantrymen occupying a pill box at the west bank of the Rhine'. This was the western abutment of the railway bridge at Breisach and the ramp above leads to the blown bridge. The three men belonged to the 30th Infantry Regiment, 3rd Division. Remarkably, though they occupied this sector for four years, the Germans left the French inscriptions inscribed on this casemate in 1940: a bellicose 'Cats are watching their prey!', and a more personal thought 'Life is beautiful, women are rare'. (USNA)

19. Armee losses between January 20 and February 5 to 800 dead, 2,596 wounded and 3,129 missing. The late orders to evacuate had saved probably 10,000 troops of all types, no more, and at least a part of their artillery, anti-tank guns and vehicles, but over 17,000 men had been taken prisoner.

On the Allied side, the 6th Army Group staff estimated American casualties around 8,000 and French twice that number. About 500 Americans had been killed in action. The toll taken by the weather on the Allied forces was also very high, one third of the losses being from non-combat injuries.

Almost as a symbol for the great opportunity lost in Alsace, a French soldier stands guard at the western end of the blown road bridge over the Rhine at Strasbourg. (ECPAD)